Research Methodology and Data Analysis

www.novapublishers.com

Research Methodology and Data Analysis

E-Records Integrity Requirements
Orlando López
2022. ISBN: 978-1-68507-553-8 (Hardcover)
2022. ISBN: 978-1-68507-726-6 (eBook)

Predictive Analytics for Data Driven Decision Making – Tools and Techniques for Solving Real World Problems
B. Uma Maheswari, PhD, L. Ashok Kumar, PhD and R. Sujatha, PhD
2022. ISBN: 978-1-68507-650-4 (Hardcover)
2022. ISBN: 978-1-68507-770-9 (eBook)

Top 10 Challenges of Big Data Analytics
Maria José Sousa, PhD and Manuel Au-Yong Oliveira (Editors)
2021. ISBN: 978-1-53619-133-2 (Hardcover)
2021. ISBN: 978-1-53619-189-9 (eBook)

Validation of Instruments for the Investigation of Sexuality in Vulnerable Groups
Lubia del Carmen Castillo Arcos (Editor)
2020. ISBN: 978-1-53618-340-5 (Hardcover)
2020. ISBN: 978-1-53618-471-6 (eBook)

Statistical Modelling of Complex Correlated and Clustered Data Household Surveys in Africa
Ngianga-Bakwin Kandala, PhD and Lawrence Kazembe, PhD (Editors)
2019. ISBN: 978-1-53615-981-3 (Hardcover)
2019. ISBN: 978-1-53615-982-0 (eBook)

More information about this series can be found at
https://novapublishers.com/product-category/series/research-methodology-and-data-analysis/

Cem Ufuk Baytar, PhD
Editor

The Future of Data Mining

Copyright © 2022 by Nova Science Publishers, Inc.
DOI: https://doi.org/10.52305/KCIN5931

All rights reserved. No part of this book may be reproduced, stored in a retrieval system or transmitted in any form or by any means: electronic, electrostatic, magnetic, tape, mechanical photocopying, recording or otherwise without the written permission of the Publisher.

We have partnered with Copyright Clearance Center to make it easy for you to obtain permissions to reuse content from this publication. Simply navigate to this publication's page on Nova's website and locate the "Get Permission" button below the title description. This button is linked directly to the title's permission page on copyright.com. Alternatively, you can visit copyright.com and search by title, ISBN, or ISSN.

For further questions about using the service on copyright.com, please contact:
Copyright Clearance Center
Phone: +1-(978) 750-8400   Fax: +1-(978) 750-4470   E-mail: info@copyright.com

NOTICE TO THE READER

The Publisher has taken reasonable care in the preparation of this book, but makes no expressed or implied warranty of any kind and assumes no responsibility for any errors or omissions. No liability is assumed for incidental or consequential damages in connection with or arising out of information contained in this book. The Publisher shall not be liable for any special, consequential, or exemplary damages resulting, in whole or in part, from the readers' use of, or reliance upon, this material. Any parts of this book based on government reports are so indicated and copyright is claimed for those parts to the extent applicable to compilations of such works.

Independent verification should be sought for any data, advice or recommendations contained in this book. In addition, no responsibility is assumed by the Publisher for any injury and/or damage to persons or property arising from any methods, products, instructions, ideas or otherwise contained in this publication.

This publication is designed to provide accurate and authoritative information with regard to the subject matter covered herein. It is sold with the clear understanding that the Publisher is not engaged in rendering legal or any other professional services. If legal or any other expert assistance is required, the services of a competent person should be sought. FROM A DECLARATION OF PARTICIPANTS JOINTLY ADOPTED BY A COMMITTEE OF THE AMERICAN BAR ASSOCIATION AND A COMMITTEE OF PUBLISHERS.

Additional color graphics may be available in the e-book version of this book.

Library of Congress Cataloging-in-Publication Data

ISBN: 979-8-88697-250-4

Published by Nova Science Publishers, Inc. † New York

Contents

Preface vii

Acknowledgments ix

Chapter 1   **Data Analytics Applied to the Human Resources Industry** 1
Cem Ufuk Baytar

Chapter 2   **Toxicogenomics Data Mining as a Promising Prioritization Tool in Toxicity Testing** 13
Katarina Živančević, Dragica Bozic, Katarina Baralić and Danijela Đukić-Ćosić

Chapter 3   **Applications of Data Mining Algorithms for Customer Recommendations in Retail Marketing** 29
Elif Delice, Lütviye Özge Polatlı, İrem Düzdar Argun and Hakan Tozan

Chapter 4   **Analysis of Customer Churn in the Banking Industry Using Data Mining** 51
Özge Doğuç

Chapter 5   **The Crowdsourcing Concept-Based Data Mining Approach Applied in Prosumer Microgrids** 77
B. C. Neagu, M. Gavrilaș, O. Ivanov and G. Grigoraș

Chapter 6   **Active Learning** 95
Jože M. Rožanec, Blaž Fortuna and Dunja Mladenić

Chapter 7	**Prediction of General Anxiety Disorder Using Machine Learning Techniques** 119
	Kevser Şahinbaş

Editor's Contact Information 139

Index 141

Preface

The purpose of this book is to discuss data mining, which is a subset of data science, from a variety of perspectives. With the technological advances of recent years, new software and hardware-based systems are available in most business environments. With these systems, data production continues to increase in personal, corporate, commercial and many other areas. Information systems convert raw data, which alone are not so meaningful, into information after the processes are applied. Database systems are necessary for the storage and management of the information generated. Revealing meaningful relationships hidden in a stack of high-volume data shows the function of data mining. Processing big data has become important to produce information that will support business decisions and be a strategic tool in today's competitive environment. In this context, the effectiveness of data mining applications is increasing day by day as a decision support system to develop marketing strategies in every sector by identifying customer behavior and target groups.

The wide perspective of book chapters is likely to provide a rich source of information for those interested in broadening their understanding of the multiple facets associated with data mining. The primary audience for this book includes business professionals, practitioners, data scientists as well as researchers who dedicate their work to issues associated with data mining (or data science). An important motivation for editing this book was the need to create an organized framework for providing various points of view about the future of data mining.

Chapter 1 provides details about the relationship between the concept of analytics and the field of human resources. It also explains the opportunities waiting for human resources. Chapter 2 presents toxicogenomic data mining as a promising functional annotation-based prioritization tool, with a concise summary of potentially useful software and tools, including their major advantages and limitations. Chapter 3 introduces applications of data mining algorithms (decision tree and random forest) for customer recommendations in retail marketing. Chapter 4 is an analysis of customer churn in the banking industry by using different machine algorithms and creating a model on the Knime platform. Chapter 5 discusses a data mining approach applied in prosumer microgrids based on the crowdsourcing concept. Chapter 6 takes an in-depth look at the field of active learning, which is a sub-field of machine learning. Chapter 7 is about prediction of general anxiety disorder by using machine learning techniques.

Cem Ufuk Baytar
Istanbul, Turkey

August 2022

Acknowledgments

I would like to convey my appreciation to all contributors. I also offer my thanks to my colleagues and family whose support was a source of encouragement during the period when I spent hours on this project.

It is my pleasure to thank all the professionals at Nova Science Publishers with whom I enjoyed working.

Chapter 1

Data Analytics Applied to the Human Resources Industry

Cem Ufuk Baytar[*]
Management Information Systems, Istanbul Topkapı University,
Istanbul, Turkey

Abstract

The department of human resources in companies plays an active role in the architecture of a strategic workforce in terms of creating and managing human capital. It is necessary to embody its strategies with appropriate raw data and accurate analyses. Human resources management gains the feature of being a strategic partner in company management by generating strategies based on consistent measurements related to the workforce. As a result of such an approach, it has an important place in creating competition in businesses and maintaining the existence of businesses. Innovations, which emerge with the transformation of data into information, not only offer a competitive advantage to companies but also help them make better decisions. In parallel with the developments in technology, changes in the business environment force human resources management to be prepared for these changes and to transform itself with this change. In this study, the concept of analytics is discussed concerning human resources. In addition, by trying to explain the relationship between human resources and analytics concepts, the opportunities waiting for human resources are revealed. As a result, it is clear that digital transformation and developments in technology make the importance of human resources increase.

---

[*] Corresponding Author's Email: ufukbaytar@topkapi.edu.tr.

In: The Future of Data Mining
Editor: Cem Ufuk Baytar
ISBN: 979-8-88697-250-4
© 2022 Nova Science Publishers, Inc.

Keywords: data analytics, data mining, data management, human resources metrics

Introduction

With the developments in Information and Communication Technologies, data can be stored and managed by bringing it together from different sources. Today, it is possible for managers to reach and use big data with various types of technologies at any time. Since deciding is one of the most critical processes for companies, it is necessary to organize and analyze large amounts of complex data by appropriate methods for decision-makers. In this context, data analytics is a field that emerged in recent years that aims to convert raw data into information with scientific and mathematical processes and methods. It has become a very interesting topic both in academia and in the business world in a short time. There are different definitions of human resources analytics, i.e., it means using advanced statistical analyses, predictive modeling procedures, and human capital investment analysis to forecast and extrapolate "what-if" scenarios for decision-making (Falletta and Combs, 2021). This study has the following objectives: (a) improving the understanding of data analytics, (b) identifying the role of data analytics in human resources management, (c) assessing the practices of human resources analytics, and (d) discussing the study's implications and future research directions

Data Analytics

The use of analytics can be traced back to the 1910s when scientific management emerged (Mortenson, Doherty and Robinson, 2015). It can be considered as the continuation of optimization and simulation techniques that could achieve maximum output with limited resources in the 1940s (Delen and Zolbanin, 2018). At the end of the 1960s, the use of computer systems to analyze data and support decision-makers led to the use of analytics. Applications called decision support systems were used in activities such as product planning, investment portfolio management, and transportation route (Davenport and Harris, 2007). These decision support systems were named Operations Research and Management Science in general. In addition to the advanced Operations Research and Management Science models that were used in many industries and management systems in the 1970s, rule-based Expert Systems (Expert Systems) emerged (Delen and Ram, 2018). Through expert systems, direct use of computers and data involved monitoring and reporting performance rather than decision-making (Davenport and Harris, 2007). In the 1980s, the application of multiple and separate information systems gave way to integrated information systems at the enterprise level, called Enterprise Resource Planning (ERP). Relational Database Management took the place of the schemas that show the data and do not have a certain standard (Delen and Ram, 2018). Thus, data from each unit of the enterprise could be collected and brought together and each unit of the enterprise had access to this data. In the 1990s, expert information systems emerged. Business Intelligence and Information Technologies started to be used in business environments (Krishnamoorthi and Mathew, 2018). Data could then be stored centrally and holistically in data warehouses. In the late 2000s, business analytics started to be used as a very important and analytical component of Business Intelligence (Krishnamoorthi and Mathew, 2018).

In these years, Data/Text Mining, Cloud Programming, and SaaS (Software as a Service) methods have also been developed (Delen and Zolbanin, 2018). In the 2010s, the internet was largely used by mobile devices, etc. Due to its widespread use with devices (Internet of Things), the new data generation big data has started to develop rapidly. Although there are many data sources in this period, social network/media data is seen as the most interesting (Delen and Ram, 2018).

Data analytics includes a group of steps to find out trends and to get results by processing data sets. To manage the process of data analytics, various types of software and specialized systems have been used by specialists. In other words, it is a field of analyzing and managing data to extract valuable insights from data. Statistical analysis and technologies are applied in the field of data analytics. It plays a vital role to analyze business processes and improving decision-making to get a competitive advantage (Stedman, 2022). Data analytics has relationships with many disciplines, for instance, statistics, mathematics, and computer programming. To make data analysis, specialists use different techniques. Some of them are data mining, data cleansing, data transformation, data modeling, etc.

Data analytics has two general methodologies. Exploratory data analysis tries to find patterns in data whereas confirmatory data analysis uses statistical techniques to determine whether hypotheses related to the data set are true or not. There are four types of data analytics as follows (Olavsrud, 2022):

- Descriptive analytics analyses current or historical data by finding patterns to describe the present situation or situation in a specified time interval, i.e, view of business intelligence in business analytics.
- Diagnostic analytics focuses on data, generally produced by descriptive analytics, to find out cause-effect relationships related to past events.
- Predictive analytics aims to make predictions about future outcomes by using some techniques, i.e., machine learning, deep learning, forecasting, etc., based on data from descriptive and diagnostic analytics. It is generally considered a type of advanced analytics.
- Prescriptive analytics is a type of advanced analytics. It makes a suggestion of a solution to reach a specified target, for instance, machine learning, business algorithms are used in business predictive analytics.

Companies in every sector use data analytics to improve operational efficiency and increase revenues. For example, UPS has developed the Harmonized Enterprise Analytics Tool (HEAT). This tool helped to keep track of the real state of every package in the system by analyzing customer data, operational data, and planning data. In another example, Kaiser Permanente aimed to improve daily operations efficiency and customer satisfaction. To reduce waiting times in queues, the company used machine learning and artificial intelligence to manage data operations in its 39 hospitals in 2015 (Olavsrud, 2022).

There are different data analytics methods and techniques as defined below (Olavsrud, 2022):

- Regression analysis is used to understand statistically whether there is a relationship between variables and to calculate the level of relationship between them, i.e., how much social media activities may affect the amount of sales.
- Monte Carlo simulation is often used for risk analysis. Specialists make models calculate the probability of events that can not be estimated because of the side effects of some variables.
- Factor analysis is a statistical method for massive data to break into smaller parts to manage them easily. In this way, it enables to discover the hidden patterns in a huge data set. For example, factor analysis is beneficial to find out some facts about customer loyalty in business.

- Cohort analysis is a technique that is used to group datasets for analyzing data groups having common characteristics (cohorts). This is often used to understand customer segments.
- Cluster analysis is used to classify structures in a dataset into related groups (clusters). For example, insurance companies try to understand the reasons why some specified locations are related to some types of insurance.
- Time series analysis is a statistical technique that tries to find out trend analysis. Data in a series of particular time intervals is analyzed to discover trends over time. It is useful for economic and sales forecasting.
- Sentiment analysis aims to identify feelings transferred from a dataset. Some tools are used, i.e., such as natural language processing, text analysis, and computational linguistics. sentiment analysis tries to interpret qualitative data, i.e., understanding how customers feel about a brand.

The process of producing meaningful information is called information discovery because of pre-processing large volumes of data after it is stored in information systems. Data mining is one of the important steps referenced in information discovery (Yıldırım and Birant, 2018). The steps, which are included in the information discovery process, are listed as follows (Han and Kamber, 2006):

- Data cleaning: Removal of data with the highest level of noise and inconsistency
- Data integration: Connecting multiple data sources
- Data selection: Removing data, which need analysis, from the database
- Data conversion: Data collection or conversion to appropriate formats
- Data mining: Creating a data pattern by using appropriate methods
- Pattern evaluation: Identification of patterns representing information based on certain criteria
- Information representation: Representation of information by using visualization techniques

Data mining consists of methods (models) that allow hidden and meaningful patterns to be found in the data stack. These methods are divided into two groups. The first of these groups consists of predictive methods. In the other group, there are descriptive methods. The main predictive methods are classification and regression models. Descriptive methods perform definitions of patterns hidden among the data. For example, revealing whether there is a similarity between the purchasing habits of married men and single women during shopping may be an example of the descriptive model. Clustering methods and association rules are among the descriptive methods. According to Özdemir et al. (2018), in predictive methods, a model is created using data with all the details previously known. These model results are applied to unknown data to achieve the results (Özdemir et al., 2018).

The classification method is the process of adding new data to predetermined classes by applying the results to this model after the creation of a model through known data (Silahtaroğlu, 2013). In this context, regression analysis commonly used in classical statistics is a kind of classification method (Gamgan and Altunkaynak, 2017). Only numeric values are used in the regression model. Some of the classification and regression models are decision trees, artificial neural networks, genetic algorithms, k-nearest neighbor, and bayes classifiers (Cömert and Kaymaz, 2019).

Decision trees form a tree-shaped structure for decision-making (Sayad, 2022). Decision trees are made up of branches and leaves. In this context, decision nodes can be divided into two or more branches. Decision nodes are used for decision-making or classification purposes depending on the data set. Leaf nodes in decision trees represent decisions. The root node is at the top of the decision tree. To reach a decision, a specific path is traced from the root of the tree to the leaf nodes. Algorithms such as ID3, C4.5, and CART are used to create decision trees (Balaban and Kartal, 2018).

Clustering is the job of assigning data to groups of objects with similar characteristics (Ceylan et al., 2017). This analysis provides the formation of data groups with common attributes. This method plays a role in determining the correct varieties. At the same time, clustering analysis is used for different purposes such as hypothetical testing, prediction for groups of objects, and detection of contrary values. The clustering of data contributes to the analysis of the data, while it also causes the details to be overlooked. Each group has a homogeneous structure in its own right (Berkhin, 2006). There are clustering models such as K-means, Fuzzy C-Means (FCM), Kohonen Networks, Hierarchical Clustering, and so on. The similarity between the data is measured by measuring the distances of the data from each other.

One of the best-known methods for clustering is the k-means algorithm, developed by Mac Queen in 1967 (Arai and Barakbah, 2007). This algorithm is based on the idea that a midpoint can represent a cluster (Steinbach et al., 2000). The algorithm is one of those clustering algorithms that automatically create clusters from similar things and is one of those types of unsupervised learning without any reference or preliminary information. It is called k-means because it creates the k original set and the center of each set is the average of the values in the cluster (Harrington, 2012).

Human Resources Analytics

Human resources (HR) analytics is human resource management associated with data for creating views deeply on how investing in assets of human capital affects success in business based on: (a) creating revenue, (b) minimizing expenses, (c) decreasing risks, and (d) executing strategic plans. It is realized by applying statistical methods to integrated human resources, talent management, and financial and operational data. HR analytics specifically deals with the metrics of the HR function, such as time to hire, training expense per employee, and time until promotion. All these metrics are managed exclusively by human resources (Lalwani, 2022). In other words, human resource analytics is defined as the systematic identification and measurement of human stimulations according to business results (Heuvel and Bondarouk, 2016). HR analytics is segmenting the workforce and using statistical analyses and predictive modeling procedures to identify key drivers (i.e., factors and variables) and cause and effect relationships that enable and inhibit important business outcomes (Falletta and Combs, 2021). The field of converting human behavior into data and examining it is defined as people analytics. Human resources analytics covers all business processes by starting with human resources. It can also be defined as a communication tool that combines data from different sources to describe the current situation and predict future outcomes. (Fitz-Enz, 2010).

Several HR metrics contribute to business value. Based on the key performance indicators (KPI) of the organization, HR can then propose the metrics that can influence these KPIs. Common metrics tracked by HR analytics are as follows (Lalwani, 2022):

- Revenue per employee is calculated by dividing a company's revenue by the total number of employees in the company. This metric indicates the average revenue each employee generates. It is a

measure of how efficient an organization is at creating revenue by employees (Jayanthi, 2020).
- The offer acceptance rate is defined as dividing the total number of job offers by the number of accepted formal job offers given in a certain time interval. A higher rate (above 85%) means a good ratio. If it is lower, this metric can be used to re-evaluate the strategy of the company's talent acquisition (Keçecioğlu and Oktay, 2010).
- Training expenses per employee are obtained by dividing the total training expense by the total number of employees who received training. The value of this expense can be determined by measuring the training efficiency. Poor efficiency may lead HR management to re-evaluate the training expense per employee.
- Training efficiency can be measured by the analysis of various data sources, such as performance improvement, test scores, and upward transition in employees' roles in the organization after training. Measuring training efficiency can be crucial to measure the effectiveness of a training program.
- The voluntary turnover rate occurs when employees voluntarily choose to leave their jobs. It is calculated by dividing the number of employees who left voluntarily by the total number of employees in the organization. This metric can lead to the identification of gaps in the employee experience that are leading to voluntary attrition (Dursun, 2013).
- Involuntary turnover rate means termination of an employee from the related position. The rate is calculated by dividing the number of employees who left involuntarily by the total number of employees in the organization. This metric can be tied back to the recruitment strategy and used to develop a plan to improve the quality of hires to avoid involuntary turnover.
- Time to fill is the number of days between advertising a job opening and hiring someone to fill that position. By measuring the time to fill, recruiters can alter their recruitment strategy to identify areas where the most time is being spent (Anger et al., 2021).
- Time to hire is the number of days between approaching a candidate and the candidate's acceptance of the job offer. Just like time to fill, data-driven analysis of time to hire can benefit recruiters and help them improve the candidate experience to reduce this time (Jayanthi, 2020).

- Absenteeism is a productivity metric. It is measured by dividing the number of days missed by the total number of scheduled workdays. Absenteeism can offer insights into overall employee health and can also serve as an indicator of employee happiness (Anger et al., 2021).

The process of human resources analytics has some steps listed as follows: (a) Understanding the organization's business goals, (b) Identifying the metrics to be analyzed to achieve those goals, (c) Collecting and analyzing the relevant data, (d) Obtaining insights into this data, and (e) Communicating how this data affects the organization.

There are different industrial applications of human resources analytics. Some of them have been summarized as follows:

General Electric (GE) experts collected different types of data relate to working environments, i.e., from power plants to hospital equipment. GE's analytics team used this data to make the machines working within it more efficient. They stated that such business analyzes may increase productivity in the US by 1.5% and increase the average national income by 30% over 20 years (Sağıroğlu and Koç, 2017).

FedEx, which has 155,000 employees worldwide, is one of the institutions that have achieved success in human resources analytics. The company has increased its use of analytics and has become able to access all the data needed. "We're always looking at HR metrics." says Bob Bennett, FedEx Executive Vice President of Human Resources, who also said, "When evaluating our ability to support business goals, we also look at business metrics" (Hattangadi, 2019).

eQuest, a company that provides recruitment consultancy services to financial companies, found in an analysis that 175,000 dollars had been spent every year on 48 job websites, and 45 of them did not give timely feedback. In addition, the company determined the words and phrases that candidates use the most while searching and decided to change the titles and definitions of job postings accordingly. As a result, candidate traffic increased by 175% and the budget spent on job postings decreased by 50% (Doğan, 2019).

Conclusion

Human resources analytics not only activates processes in human resources management and operations of the organization but also contributes to the development of the organization, its competitiveness, and brand identity as an employer. Managing data correctly gives advantages, i.e., evaluating the level of commitment of qualified manpower to the organization, analyzing the intention to leave the job, and facilitating the management of talent by estimating the potential of an employee. It should also be taken into account that there is a need for concrete, measurable and interpretable information for determining the right strategies. In this context, HR analytics plays an important role in designing a strategic human resources approach by (a) determining HR metrics in line with the priorities of the organization, (b) tracking and evaluating these metrics periodically, and (c) strengthening the talent pool by taking measures when necessary. Based on insights given in this work, research in the future can be carried out to show the effects of human resources metrics on the decisions of human resources management.

References

Anger, O., Tessema, M., Craft, J., Tsegai, S., 2021. A framework for assessing the effectiveness of hr metrics and analytics: the case of an American healthcare institution. *Global Journal of Human Resource Management* 9(1), 1-19.

Arai, K., Barakbah, A., 2007. *Hierarchical k-means: An algorithm for centroids initialization for k-means*. Faculty of Science and Engineering, Saga University.

Balaban, M. E., Kartal, E., 2018. *Veri madenciliği ve makine öğrenmesi temel algoritmaları ve R dili ile uygulamaları*. [Data mining and machine learning basic algorithms and applications with R language.] İstabul: Çağlayan Publishing.

Berkhin, P., 2006. *A survey of clustering data mining techniques in grouping multidimensional data*. Springer Berlin Heidelberg, 25-71.

Ceylan, Z., Gürsev, S., Bulkan, S., 2017. İki aşamalı kümeleme analizi ile bireysel emeklilik sektöründe müşteri profilinin değerlendirilmesi. *Bilişim Teknolojileri Dergisi* [Evaluation of customer profile in private pension sector with two-stage cluster analysis. *Journal of Information Technologies*]10(4), 475-485.

Cömert, N., Kaymaz, M., 2019. Araç sigortası hilelerinde veri madenciliğinin kullanımı. Marmara Üniversitesi, *İktisadi ve İdari Bilimler Dergisi* [The use of data mining in car insurance cheats.] Marmara University, *Journal of Economics and Administrative Sciences*] 41(2), 364-390.

Davenport, T. H., Harris, J.G., Morison, R., 2010. *Analytics at Work: Smarter Decisions, Better Results*. Boston: Harvard Business Press.

Delen, D., Ram, S., 2018. Research Challenges and Opportunities in Business Analytics. *Journal of Business Analytics* 1(1), 2-12.

Delen, D., Zolbanin, H.M., 2018. the Analytics Paradigm in Business Research. *Journal of Business Research* 90, 186-195.

Doğan, G., 2019. *Büyük Veri İnsan Kaynaklarına Ne Sunuyor?* [*What Does Big Data Offer to Human Resources?*] https://kaynakbaltas.com/kultur/buyuk-veri-insan-kaynaklarina-ne-sunuyor/.

Dursun, B., 2013. *İnsan Kaynakları Yönetimi*. [*Human Resources Management*] Istanbul: Beta publishing house.

Falletta, S.V., Combs, W. L., 2021. The HR analytics cycle: a seven-step process for building evidence-based and ethical HR analytics capabilities. *Journal of Work-Applied Management* 13(1), 51-68.

Fitz-Enz, J., Mattox, J., 2014. *Predictive Analytics for Human Resources*. New Jersey: Wiley and SAS Business Series.

Gamgam, H., Altunkaynak, B., 2017. *SPSS uygulamalı regresyon analizi* [*SPSS applied regression analysis*]. (2 ed.).

Han, J., Kamber, M., 2006. *Data mining concepts and techniques*. San Francisco: Elsevier, Morgan Kaufmann Publishers.

Harrington, P., 2012. *Machine learning in action*. Manning Publications Co.

Hattangadi, V., 2019. *Firms are turning to people analytics to achieve better efficiencies*. https://www.financialexpress.com/opinion/firms-are-turning-to-people-analytics-to-achieve-better-efficiencies/1734443/

Heuvel, S., Bondarouk, T., 2016. The Rise (and Fall) of HR Analytics: A Study into the Future Applications, Value, Structure, and System Support. *Journal of Organizational Effectiveness People and Performance* 4(2), 127-148.

Jayanthi, R., 2020. A Study on Effectiveness of HR Metrics. *International Journal of Science and Research (IJSR)* 9(2), 1630-1635.

Keçecioğlu, T., Oktay, S., 2010. İnsan Sermayesinin Sayısallaştırılmasının Dayanılmaz Çekim Gücü [The Irresistible Attraction of the Digitization of Human Capital]. *Dokuz Eylül Üniversitesi, Sosyal Bilimler Enstitüsü Dergisi* [*Journal of Social Sciences Institute*] 12(3), 67-86.

Krishnamoorthi, S., Mathew, S.K., 2018. Business analytics and business value: A comparative case study. *Information & Management* 55(5), 643-666.

Lalwani, P., 2022. *What Is HR Analytics? Definition, Importance, Key Metrics, Data Requirements, and Implementation*. Accessed June 20. https://www.spiceworks.com/hr/hr-analytics/articles/what-is-hr-analytics/.

Mortenson, M. J., Doherty, N. F., Robinson, S., 2015. Operational Research from Taylorism to Terabytes: A Research Agenda for the Analytics Age. *European Journal of Operational Research*, 241(3), 583-595.

Olavsrud, T., 2022. *What is data analytics? Analyzing and managing data for decisions*. Accessed June 15. https://www.cio.com/article/191313/what-is-data-analytics-analyzing-and-managing-data-for-decisions.html.

Özdemir, A., Sağlam, R., Bilen, B. B., 2018. Eğitim Sisteminde Veri Madenciliği Uygulamaları ve Farkındalık Üzerine Bir Durum Çalışması. *Atatürk Üniversitesi Sosyal Bilimler Enstitüsü Dergisi* [A Case Study on Data Mining Applications and Awareness in Education System. *Journal of Atatürk University Institute of Social Sciences*] 22 (Özel Sayı), 2159-2172.

Sağıroğlu, Ş., Koç, O., 2017. *Büyük Veri ve Açık Veri Analitiği: Yöntemler ve Uygulamalar*. Ankara: Grafiker publishing house.

Sayad, S., 2022. *Decision tree regression*. Accessed May 1 https://www.saedsayad.com/decision_tree_reg.htm.

Stedman, C., 2022. *Data analytics (DA)*. Accessed June 2 https://www.techtarget.com/searchdatamanagement/definition/data-analytics.

Silahtaroğlu, G., 2013. *Veri Madenciliği Kavram ve Algoritmaları*. [Data Mining Concepts and Algorithms.] Papatya publisher.

Steinbach, M., Karypis, G., Kumar, V., 2000. A comparison of document clustering techniques. *The sixth ACM SIGKDD International Conference on Knowledge Discovery and Data Mining*.

Yıldırım, P., Birant, D., 2018. Bulut bilişimde veri madenciliği tekniklerinin uygulanması: Bir literatür taraması. *Pamukkale Üniv Muh Bilim Dergisi* [Application of data mining techniques in cloud computing: A literature review. *Pamukkale University Journal of Muh Science*] 24(2), 336-343.

Chapter 2

Toxicogenomics Data Mining as a Promising Prioritization Tool in Toxicity Testing

Katarina Živančević[1,2,†]**, Dragica Bozic**[1,†]**,
Katarina Baralić**[1,†] **and Danijela Đukić-Ćosić**[1,*]

[1]Department of Toxicology "Akademik Danilo Soldatović,"
University of Belgrade - Faculty of Pharmacy, Belgrade, Serbia
[2]Institute of Physiology and Biochemistry "Ivan Đaja,"
University of Belgrade - Faculty of Biology, Belgrade, Serbia

Abstract

Within regulatory agencies and toxicological research teams, there is an increasing interest in developing, testing, and using novel techniques, such as -omics, to analyse chemical risks even more efficiently. Toxicogenomics explores the connections between genes and environmental stress in disease aetiology by combining measurements of families of biomolecules with bioinformatics and traditional toxicology. It has a potential to predict gene functions within specific biological pathways, identify genomic biomarkers and reduce gene sets. Furthermore, it provides mixture evaluation techniques, taking into account all the potential chemical, gene, protein, metabolite, and network interactions that may be significant in triggering mixture toxicities (antagonistic, additive/synergistic action). Hence, toxicogenomics data mining might be viewed as an important stepping stone for further *in vitro* and *in vivo* analyses, enabling the reduction of time and cost of the overall analysis, as well as the number of laboratory animals, in accordance with the animal welfare and the 3R principle. Having all of

---

[*] Corresponding Author's Email: danijela.djukic.cosic@pharmacy.bg.ac.rs.
[†] The authors have equally contributed the research.

In: The Future of Data Mining
Editor: Cem Ufuk Baytar
ISBN: 979-8-88697-250-4
© 2022 Nova Science Publishers, Inc.

this in mind, in this chapter, toxicogenomics data mining will be presented as a promising functional annotation-based prioritization tool, with a concise summary of potentially useful software and tools, including their major advantages and limitations.

Keywords: bioinformatics, database, software, tools, *in silico*

Introduction

Traditional toxicological approaches, such as animal research, are limited by cost, time, and ethical considerations (Basile et al., 2019; Prior et al., 2019). With the goal of reducing animal testing by 2035, the US Environmental Protection Agency (EPA) proposed *in silico* modeling for assessing multiple toxicity end-points of the tested chemicals (Kar and Leszczynski, 2020), recommending the application of numerous computational techniques capable of analyzing, simulating, visualizing, or predicting toxicity (Myatt et al., 2018). *In silico* models are extremely complicated, relying on the information obtained by statistics, mathematics, bioinformatics, biochemistry, and molecular biology (Đukić-Ćosić et al., 2021; Shegokar, 2020). Furthermore, massive amounts of toxicity data have been accumulated in numerous databases during the last few decades. In most cases, they are used to access experimental data in a convenient manner and contain experimental evidence that may serve as a foundation for the development of new scientific hypotheses (Helma et al., 2000). High-throughput toxicity screening tests are considered capable of replacing many previously used *in vivo* tests, with non-profit organizations, regulatory agencies (EPA, Health Canada, European Chemicals Agency-ECHA), and international organizations (Organization for Economic Cooperation and Development-OECD) advocating for this change and promoting initiatives to reduce the amount of required animal-based tests (Oki and Edwards, 2016). Toxicogenomic methods, which may include not only genomics, but also transcriptomics, proteomics, metabolomics, and epigenomics, seek to understand molecular causes of toxicity from a holistic point of view. Most often, their additional goal is to identify expression patterns (i.e., biomarkers) with aim to predict toxicity or genetic vulnerability to toxic substances. This discipline has progressed as a result of improvements in mechanistic toxicology, toxicity evaluations efficiency, chemical safety assessments, and novel drug development tests (Koedrith et al., 2013). It has a potential to add value in predicting gene functions within specific biological pathways, as well as in reducing gene sets (Baralić et al., 2022). Furthermore, it provides mixture evaluation techniques, taking into account all the potential chemical, gene, protein, metabolite, and network interactions that may be significant in triggering mixture toxicities (antagonistic, additive/synergistic action) (Baralić et al., 2021a; Živančević et al., 2021). Hence, toxicogenomics data mining might be viewed as an important stepping stone for further *in vitro* and *in vivo* analysis, enabling the reduction of time and cost of the overall analysis, as well as the number of laboratory animals, in accordance with the animal welfare and the 3R principle (Bozic et al., 2022).

Having all of this in mind, in this chapter, toxicogenomics data mining will be presented as a promising functional annotation-based prioritization tool, with a concise summary of potentially useful software and tools, including their major strength and limitations.

Useful Databases and Tools for Data Mining in Toxicology

The rapid advance in toxicogenomics has led to the development of distinct computational tools that can facilitate the use of publicly available data for toxicology research in compliance with the 3R principle. Here, we will mention some of the most frequently used databases, together with the tools for their analysis.

Comparative Toxicogenomic Database (CTD; http://ctdbase.org/) is a public resource integrated with the data from OMIM, MeSH, NCBI Gene, GO, KEGG and Reactome Pathway databases, developed with the aim to capture the information on chemicals, genes and molecular mechanisms behind chemically-induced diseases (Grondin et al., 2021). Firstly, CTD focused on chemical-gene, chemical-disease, and gene-disease interactions. However, over the last decade, it has evolved and developed, capturing new curation paradigms such as chemical-exposure statements and chemical-phenotype interactions (Davis et al., 2020). Currently, CTD contains more than 2.6 million of manually curated interactions for almost 17 000 chemicals, more than 53 000 genes, and 7,267 diseases extracted from 139,720 carefully revised references (http://ctdbase.org/about/dataStatus.go).

In the field of toxicology, the application of CTD has become a powerful tool for predicting potentially hazardous effects of a given molecule or even mixtures (Boverhof and Zacharewski, 2006). The aim of capturing chemical(s) interacting genes is to further assess the ability of a given chemical to induce or reduce the expression of protein-coding genes, protein synthesis and/or secretion, which might suggest the ability of the investigated chemical to disrupt different molecular pathways/processes in the organism (Cronin et al., 2009; Živančević et al., 2019).

The in-depth understanding of the selected gene-data can be achieved by the integration of the data from CTD with other mining tools/databases such as ToppGene Suite, The Database for Annotation, Visualization and Integrated Discovery (DAVID), DisGeNET or Cytoscape, open source platform for visualization of complex networks and their integration with any type of attribute data.

ToppGene Suite (https://toppgene.cchmc.org/) is a publicly available website that can be used for gene list functional enrichment and candidate gene prioritization. This is accomplished by using either functional annotations or network analysis, identification and prioritization of novel candidate genes in interactome, a protein-protein interaction network (Chen et al., 2009). This is particularly useful for gaining the mechanistic knowledge of substance-induced toxicity or adverse outcome. Similarly, DAVID (https://david.ncifcrf.gov/) was developed with an idea to provide a comprehensive set of functional annotation tools used for elucidating biological meaning of genes. Users can easily add large gene-lists, change background populations, select species and categories and reset functional parameters for data analysis. Simultaneous application of all available tools during the analysis is also possible, as well as formatting the final output (Jiao et al., 2012). In other words, DAVID facilitates the transition from genome-scale datasets collection to biological meaning (Dennis et al., 2003).

Another useful resource designed as the largest publicly available collection of genes and variants associated to human diseases is DisGeNET (https://www.disgenet.org/). The current version of DisGeNET (v7.0) contains 1,134,942 gene-disease associations, curated for 21,671 genes and 30,170 diseases, disorders, traits, and clinical or abnormal human phenotypes. Moreover, 369,554 variant-disease associations between almost 195,000 variants and more than 14,000 diseases, traits, and phenotypes are described in the latest version (Piñero et al., 2020). Thus, combining CTD data-mining with DisGeNET can be viewed as a useful way for predicting chemically-induced abnormal human phenotypes (Baralić et al., (2022)).

Finally, one of the most famous software used for the genome-related biological research is Cytoscape - a network visualization tool integrated with different plug-ins (Shannon et al., 2003). For example, GeneMANIA plug-in can be used for identification of the genes most related to a query gene set by using a guilt-by-association approach (Montojo et al., 2014), while

CytoHubba uses several topological algorithms to explore the most important nodes/hubs and fragile motifs in the generated network. The advantage of this plug-in is to prioritize and predict essential genes/proteins in complex biological networks (Chin et al., 2014). For example, Uddin and Wang (2022) were able to discover the key tumor-stroma associated biomarkers which correlated with dysregulated pathways, tumor immunity, tumor progression, and clinical outcomes in breast cancer by exploring the hub genes, oncogenes and protein kinases (Uddin et al., 2020). On the other hand, ClueGo is used for single and comparison cluster analysis that can be considered helpful for identification of pathways regulated by gene sets obtained by *in silico* and/or experimental analyses. ClueGo is updated with the newest files from Gene Ontology, KEGG, WikiPathways and Reactome. Its functionality is improved by CluePedia, which calculates linear and non-linear statistical dependencies of genes, proteins and miRNAs integrated into a network with ClueGO terms/pathways (Bindea et al., 2013).

Data Mining Examples

As an example, Davis et al., (2008) presented data mining using arsenic as an example. They demonstrated how CTD can be applied as an insight into the biological functions and molecular networks affected by the exposure to arsenic, including stress response, apoptosis, cell cycle, and specific protein signaling pathways. Integrating arsenic-gene data with gene-disease data provided a list of diseases connected to arsenic exposure, as well as a list of genes that may explain this association (Davis et al., 2008).

Other studies also used this *in silico* approach to explore metal-induced toxic effects. In a study conducted by Živančević et al., (2021), CTD and Cytoscape software were utilized to examine the impact of environmentally relevant toxic metals (lead, methylmercury (organic form of mercury), cadmium, and arsenic) on molecular pathways implicated in the development of amyotrophic lateral sclerosis (ALS), Parkinson's disease (PD), and Alzheimer's disease (AD). The findings revealed 7, 13, and 14 genes common to all the tested metals and related to ALS, PD, and AD, respectively, while SOD2 gene was highlighted as the most important mutual gene for all the selected diseases. The primary identified biochemical pathways involved in the development of the investigated neurodegenerative disorders were oxidative stress, folate metabolism, vitamin B12, AGE-RAGE, and apoptosis. The examined metal mixture was also found to influence various biological processes. Glutathione metabolic process was listed as the most important for ALS, cellular response to toxic substance for PD, and neuron death for AD (Živančević et al., 2021).

In order to develop a feasible set of genomic biomarkers, Baralić et al., (2022) used *in silico* toxicogenomic data mining to investigate the link between phthalates and bisphenol A (BPA) co-exposure and obesity, as well as its comorbid conditions. For this purpose, CTD database was used as the main *in silico* tool, along with GeneMania, ToppGene Suite and DisGeNET. As a result, 7 mutual genes (6 relevant to humans: CCL2, IL6, LPL, PPARG, SERPINE1, and TNF) were identified in all the investigated obesity comorbidities. Additionally, of all the extracted genes, PPARG and LPL were found most closely linked to obesity (Baralić et al., 2022). The same group of authors investigated the connections between DEHP, DBP and BPA co-exposure and type 2 diabetes mellitus (T2DM), male infertility and asthma (Baralić et al., 2021a, 2021b, 2021c). In the aforementioned studies, CTD and ToppGene Suite were used as the main data mining tools, along with the Cytoscape software. The analysis revealed 44, 20 and 24 genes common to all the investigated substances and involved in the development of T2DM, male infertility and asthma, respectively. Apoptosis and oxidative stress were singled out as the most important mechanisms of both DMT2 and asthma (Baralić et al., 2021a, 2021c), while inflammation was additionally highlighted as a particularly important pathway in asthma development (Baralić et al., 2021a). Proposed mechanisms of DEHP, DBP and BPA mixture induced testicular toxicity were effects on sex differentiation, metabolism, nuclear receptors, aryl hydrocarbon receptors, apoptosis, and oxidative stress (Baralić et al., 2021b). Since oxidative stress was highlighted as one of the main mechanisms of phthalate and BPA mixture for of all of these disorders, data mining results were further validated by additional *in vivo* experiments, further suggesting additive effects of the investigated substances (Baralić et al., 2021a, 2021b, 2021c).

Another study which combined *in silico* with *in vivo* results was performed by Dong et al., (2018). As a follow-up to the *in vivo* zebrafish experiment, these authors performed CTD data mining for BPA and DBP. In their study, by conducting CTD analysis, they discovered 4826 and 14737 interactions with various genes/proteins for DBP and BPA, respectively. When orthologous human genes in BPA- and DBP-treated embryos were compared to curated BPA- and DBP-interacting proteins in CTD, 18 and 13 mutual proteins were found, respectively, while 7 and 9 of the 18 and 13 proteins were part of the BPA- and DBP-predicted pathways, respectively.

The results of CTD and proteomic analysis further highlighted the possible impacts of BPA and DBP on the hypothesized networks (Dong et al., 2018).

Furthermore, Baralić et al., (2020) assessed both risks and benefits of the COVID-19 treatment with candidate drug combinations: lopinavir/ritonavir and chloroquine/hydroxychloroquine + azithromycin, by using CTD, Cytoscape software and ToppGene Suite portal as a foundation in their research. Lopinavir/ritonavir increased the expression of specific genes involved in the immune response and lipid metabolism (IL6, ICAM1, CCL2, TNF, APOA1, etc.). Chloroquine/hydroxychloroquine + azithromycin interacted with six genes (CCL2, CTSB, CXCL8, IL1B, IL6 and TNF), whereas chloroquine + azithromycin acted on two extra genes (BCL2L1 and CYP3A4) (Baralić et al., 2020).

Using the immunomodulator sulforaphane (SFN) as a case study, Bozic et al., (2021) applied toxicogenomic data mining (CTD, ToppGene Suite portal and Reactome Knowledgebase) to investigate molecular mechanisms and pathways which might be targeted in cancer treatment. Sulforaphane interacted with 1896 different proteins, the most important being NFE2L2, NQO1, HMOX1, GCLC, TXNRD1, IL1B, IFNG, AGT, KEAP1, and CASP3. A direct evidence was found in CTD that SFN interacted with a total of 169 genes connected to its therapeutic effect against various forms of cancer, including hepatocellular carcinoma, colorectal neoplasms, uterine cervical neoplasms, and adenomatous polyposis coli (Bozic et al., 2021). The same group of authors further explored SFN induced adverse effects in colorectal carcinoma patients. In this study, gene network analysis was performed using Cytoscape plug-in STRING. Functional annotation clustering was performed by the Cytoscape plug-in BINGO, while SFN interacting genes were obtained from CTD. SFN was found to increase the expression of TIMP1, AURKA, and CEP55, and decrease the expression of CRYAB, PLCE1, and MMP28, which may contribute to the advancement of colorectal carcinoma (CTD). According to the pathway enrichment analyses, SFN enhanced RUNX2 and AURKA activation through TPX2 and IL-10 signaling (Bozic et al., 2022).

Advantages

Conventional toxicity testing and human health risk assessment strategies offer limited insight into the fundamental molecular mechanisms that contribute to adverse outcomes (Chepelev et al., 2015). In order to improve and facilitate risk assessment of thousands of chemicals with insufficient toxicity data, significant adjustment of the conventional approach is required (Chepelev et al., 2015). Since toxicogenomics explores the connections between genes and environmental stress in disease aetiology by combining measurements of families of biomolecules with bioinformatics and traditional toxicology, it has a potential to add value in predicting gene functions within specific biological pathways, as well as to identify genomic biomarkers and reduce gene sets (Boverhof and Zacharewski, 2006; Breda et al., 2014; Liu et al., 2020; Tung et al., 2020). In the light of this, toxicogenomics biomarkers are of particular importance having in mind that they can be discovered earlier than histopathological or clinical phenotypes (Ulrich and Friend, 2002). Furthermore, toxicogenomic approach enables high-throughput screening of toxic substances, which could lead to facilitated prioritization of chemicals in toxicity testing (Franzosa et al., 2021). Moreover, combining toxicogenomics with other bioinformatics approaches, such as cheminformatics, could facilitate rapid prediction of the pharmacokinetic and physicochemical key parameters for examined molecules and, thus, provide integrated data sets which could be used in regulatory purposes (Daina et al., 2017). Toxicogenomics approaches could also facilitate adverse outcome pathways (AOP) development and enhance read-across strategies (Liu et al., 2020). AOP is a conceptual framework which connects molecular initiating events and key events with outcomes and adverse effects in risk assessment (Sewell et al., 2018). It integrates molecules, gene activities, and causal adverse outcomes. In this context, toxicogenomics represents an important resource for linking the information among the AOP components (key events and their relationships) (Liu et al., 2020). On the other hand, read-across assumes that the two 'similar' compounds are likely to share a similar toxicity profile based on their structural similarities (Liu et al., 2020). However, if the two chemicals have similar biological profiles, they might also share an adverse outcome (Liu et al., 2020). Thus, diverse biological data, including toxicogenomic, could also be used for biological fingerprint profiling of chemicals. Thus, biologically-based read-across could be viewed as a complement to the structure-based read-across (Ball et al., 2016). Toxicogenomic data also offers strategies to derive molecular points of departure (POD) for the dose-response assessment (Phillips et al., 2015). Exposure to mixtures of toxic substances that are not entirely known is a plausible scenario which should be explored in occupational or environmental toxicology (Martins et al., 2019). Conveniently, toxicogenomics also provides mixture evaluation techniques, taking into consideraton all the potential chemical, gene, protein, metabolite, and network interactions that may be important in triggering mixture toxicities

(Altenburger et al., 2012). Furthermore, this discipline could help to distinguish the concept of interactions between toxic substances (antagonistic, additive/synergistic) (Martins et al., 2019). Finally, it allows the prediction of potential long-term effects of exposures, enabling the reduction of time and cost of the overall analysis, as well as the number of laboratory animals, in accordance with the animal welfare and the 3R principle (Yauk et al., 2019). Hence, toxicogenomics data mining might be viewed as an important stepping stone for further *in vitro*, *in vivo* and human biomonitoring research.

Limitations

Although toxicogenomics approach is a promising functional annotation-based prioritization tool, its major limitations should not be overlooked. Online sources (i.e., CTD, GeneMANIA plug-in, ToppGene Suite portal, etc.) rely on limited available data and, therefore, the quality of the analysis depends on the data relevance (Chen et al., 2009; Živančević et al., 2021). Due to the fact that conclusions based on toxicogenomic data mining imply drawing statistical associations between chemical-gene-disease relationships, it is not possible to take into consideration some important aspects, such as dose-response relationship, route and duration of exposure to chemicals, along with the individual sensitivity of exposed subjects (Davis et al., 2009). The main challenge of utilization of toxicogenomic data for risk assessment applications is the lack of internationally harmonized rules for toxicogenomic experimental methods, quality standards, references, and analytical frameworks that provide the criteria and standards required for global consistency (Vachon et al., 2017; Yauk et al., 2019). Additionally, the lack of internationally approved strategies or frameworks for applying toxicogenomics in specific risk assessment, as well as the lack of expertise and training in toxicogenomics within the regulatory community in certain areas, represent a challenge in applying toxicogenomics data in the regulatory purposes (Pain et al., 2020; Yauk et al., 2019). Inadequate regulatory capability to evaluate provided toxicogenomic data, as well as limited applicability to certain areas are also issues which need to be addressed and resolved (Yauk et al., 2019). Incomplete validation of pathway alterations in specific diseases, or incomplete validation of the observed changes in gene expression are proportional to the severity of the adverse effect (Yauk et al., 2019). Also, the lack of high-quality toxicogenomic data make its integration in toxicity testing impossible (Krewski et al., 2020; Yauk et al., 2019).

Some of the challenges in the mixture toxicity analysis are that detected signals must be linked to the predefined response chains. It is also necessary to understand the crosstalk and convergence of the pathways, considering that joint responses might switch between independent and concentration additive, or non-interactive and interactive. Since quantitative mixture assessment typically relies on monotonous changes in response represented in sigmoidal concentration response relationships, U-shaped curves present specific challenges (Altenburger et al., 2012). Elucidation of the sequences of biological responses, as well as separation of toxicokinetic from toxicodynamic responses could also represent a challenge in interpretation of toxicogenomic data (Altenburger et al., 2012). "Omics" techniques, are generally complex to compute and understand. Thus, toxicogenomics data mining could be demanding, especially in the integration of different data formats (Martins et al., 2019), especially considering the variability of available data and measured endpoints (Liu et al., 2020). The reproducibility of toxicogenomic data, including both biological and technical sides, could also make drawing conclusions difficult (Liu et al., 2020). Applicability domain of toxicogenomic data is also an important factor which may limit the analysis. A false positive result could be generated by biologically-based read-across, which relies on toxicogenomic data (Liu et al., 2020). The fast development of toxicogenomic approach has greatly expanded its impact on toxicity data testing. However, aforementioned challenges should be addressed before toxicogenomic data mining can meet its full potential as a promising prioritization tool in toxicity testing (Liu et al., 2020).

Conclusion

The use of bioinformatic data mining methods in toxicology is growing, and various *in silico* toxicity prediction tools and databases are updated on a regular basis to meet the customer demands. In this chapter, toxicogenomics data mining was marked as a prospective functional annotation-based prioritizing approach, while its primary advantages and limitations were addressed. All things considered, toxicogenomics data mining might be seen as a useful tool for predicting and providing better understanding of complicated mechanisms of toxicity, identifying genomic biomarkers, reducing gene sets and evaluating mixtures of toxic substances. Finally, it can be viewed as a valuable prioritization tool for further laboratory investigations, allowing a decrease in total time and expense, as well as the number of laboratory animals.

Acknowledgments

Ministry of Education, Science and Technological Development of the Republic of Serbia in the framework of scientific cooperation with the People's Republic of China (451-03-1203/2021-09).

References

Altenburger, R., Scholz, S., Schmitt-Jansen, M., Busch, W., Escher, B. I., 2012. Mixture toxicity revisited from a toxicogenomic perspective. *Environmental Science and Technology* 46, 2508-2522. https://doi.org/10.1021/es2038036.

Ball, N., Cronin, M. T. D., Shen, J., Blackburn, K., Booth, E. D., Bouhifd, M., Donley, E., Egnash, L., Hastings, C., Juberg, D. R., Maertens, A., Marty, S., Naciff, J. M., Palmer, J., Pamies, D., 2016. Toward Good Read-Across Practice (GRAP) Guidance. *Altex* 33, 149-166.

Baralić, K., Bozic, D., Živančević, K., Milenković, M., Javorac, D., Marić, Đ., Miljaković, E. A., Djordjevic, A. B., Vukomanović, P., Ćurčić, M., Bulat, Z., Antonijević, B., Đukić-Ćosić, D., 2021a. Integrating in silico with *in vivo* approach to investigate phthalate and bisphenol A mixture-linked asthma development: Positive probiotic intervention. *Food and Chemical Toxicology* 158, 112671. https://doi.org/10.1016/j.fct.2021.112671.

Baralić, K., Jorgovanović, D., Živančević, K., Antonijević Miljaković, E., Antonijević, B., Buha Djordjevic, A., Ćurčić, M., Đukić-Ćosić, D., 2020. Safety assessment of drug combinations used in COVID-19 treatment: in silico toxicogenomic data-mining approach. *Toxicology and Applied Pharmacology* 406, 115237. https://doi.org/10.1016/j.taap.2020.115237.

Baralić, K., Jorgovanović, D., Živančević, K., Buha Djordjević, A., Antonijević Miljaković, E., Miljković, M., Kotur-Stevuljević, J., Antonijević, B., Đukić-Ćosić, D., 2021b. Combining *in vivo* pathohistological and redox status analysis with in silico toxicogenomic study to explore the phthalates and bisphenol A mixture-induced testicular toxicity. *Chemosphere* 267, 129296. https://doi.org/10.1016/j.chemosphere.2020.129296.

Baralić, K., Živančević, K., Božić, D., Jennen, D., Buha Djordjevic, A., Antonijević Miljaković, E., Đukić-Ćosić, D., 2022. Potential genomic biomarkers of obesity and its comorbidities for phthalates and bisphenol A mixture: In silico toxicogenomic approach. *Biocell* 46, 519-533. https://doi.org/10.32604/biocell.2022.018271.

Baralić, K., Živančević, K., Jorgovanović, D., Javorac, D., Radovanović, J., Gojković, T., Djordjevic, A. B., Ćurčić, M., Mandinić, Z., Bulat, Z., Antonijević, B., Đukić-Ćosić,

D., 2021c. Probiotic reduced the impact of phthalates and bisphenol A mixture on type 2 diabetes mellitus development: merging bioinformatics with *in vivo* analysis. *Food and Chemical Toxicology* 154, 112325. https://doi.org/10.1016/j.fct.2021.112325.

Basile, A. O., Yahi, A., Tatonetti, N. P., 2019. Artificial Intelligence for Drug Toxicity and Safety. *Trends in Pharmacological Sciences* 40, 624-635. https://doi.org/10.1016/j.tips.2019.07.005.

Bindea, G., Galon, J., Mlecnik, B., 2013. CluePedia Cytoscape plugin: Pathway insights using integrated experimental and *in silico* data. *Bioinformatics* 29, 661-663. https://doi.org/10.1093/bioinformatics/btt019.

Boverhof, D. R., Zacharewski, T. R., 2006. Toxicogenomics in risk assessment: Applications and needs. *Toxicological Sciences* 89, 352-360. https://doi.org/10.1093/toxsci/kfj018.

Bozic, D., Baralić, K., Živančević, K., Miljaković, E. A., Ćurčić, M., Antonijević, B., Djordjević, A. B., Bulat, Z., Zhang, Y., Yang, L., Đukić-Ćosić, D., 2022. Predicting sulforaphane-induced adverse effects in colon cancer patients via *in silico* investigation. *Biomedicine & Pharmacotherapy* 146, 112598. https://doi.org/10.1016/j.biopha.2021.112598.

Bozic, D., Živančević, K., Baralić, K., Javorac, D., 2021. Applying *in silico* toxicogenomic data mining to predict molecular mechanisms and pathways against carcinoma: immunomodulator sulforaphane as a case study, in: *1st International Conference on Chemo and Bioinformatics,* October 26-27, Kragujevac, Serbia. pp. 470-473.

Breda, S. G. J. Van, Claessen, S. M. H., Lo, K., Herwijnen, M. Van, Gaj, S., Kok, T. M. C. M. De, Kleinjans, J. C. S., 2014. Epigenetic mechanisms underlying arsenic - associated lung carcinogenesis. *Archives of Toxicology* 89, 1959-1969. https://doi.org/10.1007/s00204-014-1351-2.

Chen, J., Bardes, E. E., Aronow, B. J., Jegga, A. G., 2009. ToppGene Suite for gene list enrichment analysis and candidate gene prioritization. *Nucleic Acids Research* 37, 305-311. https://doi.org/10.1093/nar/gkp427.

Chepelev, N. L., Moffat, I. D., Labib, S., Bourdon-Lacombe, J., Kuo, B., Buick, J. K., Lemieux, F., Malik, A. I., Halappanavar, S., Williams, A., Yauk, C. L., 2015. Integrating toxicogenomics into human health risk assessment: Lessons learned from the benzo[a]pyrene case study. *Critical Reviews in Toxicology* 45, 44-52. https://doi.org/10.3109/10408444.2014.973935.

Chin, C. H., Chen, S. H., Wu, H. H., Ho, C. W., Ko, M. T., Lin, C. Y., 2014. cytoHubba: Identifying hub objects and sub-networks from complex interactome. *BMC Systems Biology* 8, S11. https://doi.org/10.1186/1752-0509-8-S4-S11.

Cronin, M. T. D., Bajot, F., Enoch, S. J., Madden, J. C., Roberts, D. W., Schwöbel, J., 2009. The *in chemico-in silico* interface: Challenges for integrating experimental and computational chemistry to identify toxicity. *ATLA Alternatives to Laboratory Animals* 37, 513-521. https://doi.org/10.1177/026119290903700508.

Daina, A., Michielin, O., Zoete, V., 2017. SwissADME: A free web tool to evaluate pharmacokinetics, drug-likeness and medicinal chemistry friendliness of small molecules. *Scientific Reports* 7, 1-13. https://doi.org/10.1038/srep42717.

Davis, A. P., Murphy, C. G., Rosenstein, M. C., Wiegers, T. C., Mattingly, C. J., 2008. The Comparative Toxicogenomics Database facilitates identification and understanding of chemical-gene-disease associations: arsenic as a case study. *BMC Medical Genomics* 1, 1-12. https://doi.org/10.1186/1755-8794-1-48.

Davis, A. P., Murphy, C. G., Saraceni-Richards, C. A., Rosenstein, M. C., Wiegers, T. C., Mattingly, C. J., 2009. Comparative Toxicogenomics Database: A knowledgebase and discovery tool for chemical-gene-disease networks. *Nucleic Acids Research* 37, 786-792. https://doi.org/10.1093/nar/gkn580.

Davis, A. P., Wiegers, T. C., Grondin, C. J., Johnson, R. J., Sciaky, D., Wiegers, J., Mattingly, C. J., 2020. Leveraging the comparative toxicogenomics database to fill in knowledge gaps for environmental health: A test case for air pollution-induced cardiovascular disease. *Toxicological Sciences* 177, 392-404. https://doi.org/10.1093/toxsci/kfaa113.

Dennis, G., Sherman, B. T., Hosack, D. A., Yang, J., Gao, W., Lane, H. C., Lempicki, R. A., 2003. DAVID: Database for Annotation, Visualization, and Integrated Discovery. *Genome biology* 4. https://doi.org/10.1186/gb-2003-4-9-r60.

Dong, X., Qiu, X., Meng, S., Xu, H., Wu, X., Yang, M., 2018. Proteomic profile and toxicity pathway analysis in zebra fi sh embryos exposed to bisphenol A and di- n -butyl phthalate at environmentally relevant levels. *Chemosphere* 193, 313-320. https://doi.org/10.1016/j.chemosphere.2017.11.042.

Đukić-Ćosić, D., Baralić, K., Jorgovanović, D., Živančević, K., Javorac, D., Stojilković, N., Radović, B., Marić, Đ., Ćurčić, M., Buha-Đorđević, A., Bulat, Z., Antonijević-Miljaković, E., Antonijević, B., 2021. "*In silico*" toxicology methods in drug safety assessment. *Arhiv za farmaciju* 71, 257-278. https://doi.org/10.5937/arhfarm71-32966.

Franzosa, J. A., Bonzo, J. A., Jack, J., Baker, N. C., Kothiya, P., Witek, R. P., Hurban, P., Siferd, S., Hester, S., Shah, I., Ferguson, S. S., Houck, K. A., Wambaugh, J. F., 2021. High-throughput toxicogenomic screening of chemicals in the environment using metabolically competent hepatic cell cultures. *npj Systems Biology and Applications* 7. https://doi.org/10.1038/s41540-020-00166-2.

Grondin, C. J., Davis, A. P., Wiegers, J. A., Wiegers, T. C., Sciaky, D., Johnson, R. J., Mattingly, C. J., 2021. Predicting molecular mechanisms, pathways, and health outcomes induced by Juul e-cigarette aerosol chemicals using the Comparative Toxicogenomics Database. *Current Research in Toxicology* 2, 272-281. https://doi.org/10.1016/j.crtox.2021.08.001.

Helma, C., Gottmann, E., Kramer, S., 2000. Knowledge discovery and data mining in toxicology. *Statistical Methods in Medical Research* 9, 329-358. https://doi.org/10.1177/096228020000900403.

Jiao, X., Sherman, B. T., Huang, D. W., Stephens, R., Baseler, M. W., Lane, H. C., Lempicki, R. A., 2012. DAVID-WS: A stateful web service to facilitate gene/protein list analysis. *Bioinformatics* 28, 1805-1806. https://doi.org/10.1093/bioinformatics/bts251.

Kar, S., Leszczynski, J., 2020. Open access *in silico* tools to predict the ADMET profiling of drug candidates. *Expert Opinion on Drug Discovery* 15, 1473-1487. https://doi.org/10.1080/17460441.2020.1798926.

Koedrith, P., Kim, H. L., Weon, J. Il, Seo, Y. R., 2013. Toxicogenomic approaches for understanding molecular mechanisms of heavy metal mutagenicity and carcinogenicity. *International Journal of Hygiene and Environmental Health* 216, 587-598. https://doi.org/10.1016/j.ijheh.2013.02.010.

Krewski, D., Andersen, M. E., Tyshenko, M. G., Krishnan, K., Hartung, T., Boekelheide, K., Wambaugh, J. F., Jones, D., Whelan, M., Thomas, R., Yauk, C., Barton-Maclaren, T., Cote, I., 2020. *Toxicity testing in the 21st century: progress in the past decade and future perspectives, Archives of Toxicology.* Springer Berlin Heidelberg. https://doi.org/10.1007/s00204-019-02613-4.

Liu, Z., Huang, R., Roberts, R., Tong, W., 2020. Toxicogenomics : A 2020 Vision. *Trends in Pharmacological Sciences* 40, 92-103. https://doi.org/10.1016/j.tips.2018.12.001.

Martins, C., Dreij, K., Costa, P. M., 2019. The state-of-the art of environmental toxicogenomics: Challenges and perspectives of "omics" approaches directed to toxicant mixtures. *International Journal of Environmental Research and Public Health* 16, 1-16. https://doi.org/10.3390/ijerph16234718.

Montojo, J., Zuberi, K., Rodriguez, H., Bader, G. D., Morris, Q., 2014. GeneMANIA: Fast gene network construction and function prediction for Cytoscape. *F1000Research* 3, 1-7. https://doi.org/10.12688/f1000research.4572.1.

Myatt, G. J., Ahlberg, E., Akahori, Y., Allen, D., Amberg, A., Anger, L. T., Aptula, A., Auerbach, S., Beilke, L., Bellion, P., Benigni, R., Bercu, J., Booth, E. D., Bower, D., Brigo, A., Burden, N., Cammerer, Z., Cronin, M. T. D., Cross, K. P., Custer, L., Dettwiler, M., Dobo, K., Ford, K. A., Fortin, M. C., Gad-McDonald, S. E., Gellatly, N., Gervais, V., Glover, K. P., Glowienke, S., Van Gompel, J., Gutsell, S., Hardy, B., Harvey, J. S., Hillegass, J., Honma, M., Hsieh, J. H., Hsu, C. W., Hughes, K., Johnson, C., Jolly, R., Jones, D., Kemper, R., Kenyon, M. O., Kim, M. T., Kruhlak, N. L., Kulkarni, S. A., Kümmerer, K., Leavitt, P., Majer, B., Masten, S., Miller, S., Moser, J., Mumtaz, M., Muster, W., Neilson, L., Oprea, T. I., Patlewicz, G., Paulino, A., Lo Piparo, E., Powley, M., Quigley, D. P., Reddy, M. V., Richarz, A. N., Ruiz, P., Schilter, B., Serafimova, R., Simpson, W., Stavitskaya, L., Stidl, R., Suarez-Rodriguez, D., Szabo, D. T., Teasdale, A., Trejo-Martin, A., Valentin, J. P., Vuorinen, A., Wall, B. A., Watts, P., White, A. T., Wichard, J., Witt, K. L., Woolley, A., Woolley, D., Zwickl, C., Hasselgren, C., 2018. In silico toxicology protocols. *Regulatory Toxicology and Pharmacology* 96, 1-17. https://doi.org/10.1016/j.yrtph.2018.04.014.

Oki, N. O., Edwards, S. W., 2016. An integrative data mining approach to identifying adverse outcome pathway signatures. *Toxicology* 350-352, 49-61. https://doi.org/10.1016/j.tox.2016.04.004.

Pain, G., Hickey, G., Mondou, M., Crump, D., Hecker, M., Basu, N., Maguire, S., 2020. Drivers of and obstacles to the adoption of toxicogenomics for chemical risk assessment: Insights from social science perspectives. *Environmental Health Perspectives* 128, 1-12. .https://doi.org/10.1289/EHP6500.

Phillips, J. R., Svoboda, D. L., Tandon, A., Patel, S., Mav, D., Kuo, B., Yauk, C. L., Yang, L., Thomas, R. S., Gift, J. S., Davis, J. A., Olysyzk, L., Alex, B., Paules, R. S., Parham, F., Saddler, T., Ruchir, R., Auerbach, S. S., 2015. BMDExpress 2: Enhanced transcriptomic dose- response analysis workflow. *Bioinformatics* 14, 1780-2. https://doi.org/10.1093/bioinformatics/xxxxx.

Piñero, J., Ramírez-Anguita, J. M., Saüch-Pitarch, J., Ronzano, F., Centeno, E., Sanz, F., Furlong, L. I., 2020. The DisGeNET knowledge platform for disease genomics: 2019 update. *Nucleic Acids Research* 48, D845-D855. https://doi.org/10.1093/nar/gkz1021.

Prior, H., Casey, W., Kimber, I., Whelan, M., Sewell, F., 2019. Reflections on the progress towards non-animal methods for acute toxicity testing of chemicals. *Regulatory Toxicology and Pharmacology* 102, 30-33. https://doi.org/10.1016/j.yrtph.2018.12.008.

Sewell, F., Gellatly, N., Beaumont, M., Burden, N., Currie, R., de Haan, L., Hutchinson, T. H., Jacobs, M., Mahony, C., Malcomber, I., Mehta, J., Whale, G., Kimber, I., 2018. The future trajectory of adverse outcome pathways: a commentary. *Archives of Toxicology* 92, 1657-1661. https://doi.org/10.1007/s00204-018-2183-2.

Shannon, P., Markiel, A., Ozier, O., Shannon, P., Markiel, A., Ozier, O., Baliga, N. S., Wang, J. T., Ramage, D., Amin, N., Schwikowski, B., Ideker, T., 2003. *Cytoscape : A Software Environment for Integrated Models of Biomolecular Interaction Networks* 2498-2504. https://doi.org/10.1101/gr.1239303.

Shegokar, R., 2020. Preclinical testing-Understanding the basics first, *Drug Delivery Aspects*. Elsevier Inc. https://doi.org/10.1016/b978-0-12-821222-6.00002-6.

Tung, C. W., Jen, H., Chia, C., Wang, C., Shan, S., Pinpin, W., 2020. Leveraging complementary computational models for prioritizing chemicals of developmental and reproductive toxicity concern : an example of food contact materials. *Archives of Toxicology* 1-10. https://doi.org/10.1007/s00204-019-02641-0.

Uddin, M., Mustafa, F., Rizvi, T. A., Loney, T., Suwaidi, H. Al, Al-Marzouqi, A. H. H., Eldin, A. K., Alsabeeha, N., Adrian, T. E., Stefanini, C., Nowotny, N., Alsheikh-Ali, A., Senok, A. C., 2020. SARS-CoV-2/COVID-19: Viral Genomics, Epidemiology, Vaccines, and Therapeutic Interventions. *Viruses* 12, 526. https://doi.org/10.4324/9781351118422-5.

Ulrich, R., Friend, S. H., 2002. Toxicogenomics and drug discovery: Will new technologies help us produce better drugs? *Nature Reviews Drug Discovery* 1, 84-88. https://doi.org/10.1038/nrd710.

Vachon, J., Campagna, C., Rodriguez, M. J., Sirard, M. A., Levallois, P., 2017. Barriers to the use of toxicogenomics data in human health risk assessment: A survey of Canadian risk assessors. *Regulatory Toxicology and Pharmacology* 85, 119-123. https://doi.org/10.1016/j.yrtph.2017.01.008.

Yauk, C. L., Cheung, C., Barton-Maclaren, T. S., Boucher, S., Bourdon-Lacombe, J., Chauhan, V., Gagné, M., Gillespie, Z., Halappanavar, S., Honeyman, M., Jones, S. R., Jones-McLean, E., Labib, S., MacAulay, J., Moore, J., Paquette, M., Petronella, N., Semalulu, S., Slot, A., Vespa, A., Woodland, C. L. A., 2019. Toxicogenomic applications in risk assessment at Health Canada. *Current Opinion in Toxicology* 18, 34-45. https://doi.org/10.1016/j.cotox.2019.02.005.

Živančević, K., Baralić, K., Jorgovanović, D., Buha Djordjević, A., Ćurčić, M., Antonijević Miljaković, E., Antonijević, B., Bulat, Z., Đukić-Ćosić, D., 2021. Elucidating the influence of environmentally relevant toxic metal mixture on molecular mechanisms involved in the development of neurodegenerative diseases: In silico toxicogenomic data-mining. *Environmental Research* 194. https://doi.org/10.1016/j.envres.2021.110727.

Živančević, K., Baralić, K., Jorgovanović, D., Đukić-Ćosić, D., 2019. The Comparative Toxicogenomics database: the influence of environmental chemicals on genes (*In Serbian*). *MD-Medical Data* 11(3-4):159-164.

Chapter 3

Applications of Data Mining Algorithms for Customer Recommendations in Retail Marketing

Elif Delice[1,*], Lütviye Özge Polatlı[2], İrem Düzdar Argun[3] and Hakan Tozan[4]

[1]Management Information Systems, Istanbul Topkapı University, Istanbul, Turkey
[2]Healthcare Systems Engineering, Istanbul Medipol University, Istanbul, Turkey
[3]Industrial Engineering, Düzce University, Düzce, Turkey
[4]Industrial Engineering, Istanbul Medipol University, Istanbul, Turkey

Abstract

In recent years, researchers have highlighted how large volumes of data can be transformed into information to determine customer behaviors, and data mining applications have become a major trend. It has become critical for organizations to use a tool for understanding the relationships between data to protect their marketplace by increasing customer loyalty. Thanks to data mining applications, data can be processed and transformed into information, and in this way, target audiences can be determined while developing marketing strategies. This chapter aims to increase the market share with products specific to the customer portfolio, introduce strategic marketing tools for retaining old customers, introduce effective methods for acquiring new customers, and increase the retail sales chart, based on purchasing habits of customers. The data set was collected under pandemic conditions during the COVID-19 process and analyzed to support retail businesses in their online shopping orientation. By examining the local customer base, it was assumed that

---

[*] Corresponding Author's Email: elifdelice@topkapi.edu.tr.

In: The Future of Data Mining
Editor: Cem Ufuk Baytar
ISBN: 979-8-88697-250-4
© 2022 Nova Science Publishers, Inc.

the customer group would display similar behaviors in online or tele-ordering methods, customer identification and order estimation were made to follow an effective sales policy. Segmentation was performed with data mining applications, and the grouped data were separated according to their similarities. The data set consisting of demographic characteristics and various product information of the enterprise's customers were analyzed with Decision Tree and Random Forest, which are data mining methods, the best performing algorithm in the data set was selected by comparing the performance of the methods. As a result of the findings, appropriate suggestions were given to the business to determine the purchasing tendencies of the customers and to increase the level of effectiveness in sales-marketing strategies. In this way, materials were presented to assist the enterprise in developing strategies to increase the number of sales by taking faster and more accurate action by avoiding the time and expense that would be lost by the trial-error method.

Keywords: data mining, decision trees, random forest, k-means, x-means

Introduction

Along with the developing world, globalization, which has occurred with the contribution of technology, has led to some changes on a sectoral basis and has led to an increase in competition. The most important change that has occurred is the evolution of customers' purchasing tendencies and expectations in a different direction over time. The differentiations, starting from the customer, did not only stay with the customer, but also caused different major effects in the continuation of the process with the domino effect. The most critical point in the flow is to be able to manage the effects of change by adopting an agile structure, considering the business vision and mission. An agile management style, on the other hand, is directly proportional to grasping the differences and keeping up with the change. Since the customer is at an important point, efficient management of customer relations will have a direct impact on the market share and will enable institutions to stay competitive in the emerging competitive environment (Larson and Chang, 2016). At this point, data mining methods, which are frequently encountered in applications in terms of their increasing importance and convenience in recent years, attract the attention of researchers in sectoral as well as in different fields and facilitate the management of processes.

Data mining is an analysis technique that is supported by algorithms to reveal the information hidden in large amounts of data, plays a role in predicting the future, and contains many different methods. Thus, by highlighting useful and meaningful information, it sheds light for researchers on related issues and adds efficiency to processes. At this point, service providers need to keep up with the ongoing change and use it to their advantage by extracting useful information from the big data formed to adopt an agile structure. Understanding the changing customer expectations with different data mining methods and taking steps according to the results brings companies to the fore in their own fields of activity in differentiation that starts from the customer and affects the whole process. While the methods under the umbrella of data mining are basically grouped under two headings: methods used for estimation and methods used for identification purposes, all the methods have different features and functions. With these aspects, they can answer more than one question at the same time, and they are becoming more popular day by day (Gibert et al., 2018).

In this context, it is aimed to define the customer group in the data set by using the clustering algorithms k-means and x-means. After defining the customer group, it is aimed to examine the performance of different algorithms on the data set with the support of decision tree algorithms. The most important reason for choosing such a flow is to first subject the data to a segmentation process and to give a reference point for classification in decision tree algorithms. Thus, it was desired to determine the purchasing tendencies of the customers by adding another column to the data set those states which data belongs to which cluster, and by specifying how the estimation will be made. As a result, a model that will enable the service providers to take more robust and faster action will be put forward by eliminating the time that companies will lose with trial-and-error methods.

Literature Review

Data mining has become increasingly popular in recent years, with applications in practically every industry. The most important reason for this is that all the methods under the umbrella of data mining enable to predict the future with their different functions and make processes efficient. With the spread of method applications, researchers turned their focus to this subject, thus, the number and variety of studies in the literature have increased day by day. Studies in which data mining application areas are explained have been made in a wide range from specific applications and analyzes. In some publications, the methods are examined alone, while in others, the performances of the methods are compared.

For example, Pelleg and Moore (2000) made a comparison of two different clustering algorithms by examining X-Means and K-Means methods in their study. As a result, they revealed the methodological differences of the methods discussed together with their reasons. On the other hand, Emel and Taşkın (2005) focused on sales data with the CART decision tree technique in their research, and as a result, they produced a study examining the estimation success of the related method. Similar to Pelleg and Moore, Balabantaray, Sarma and Jha (2015) compared the usage areas/differences of K-Means and K-Medoids algorithms, which are the two most used methods among descriptive data mining methods, using WEKA software. Also, Kale and Yüksel (2020) conducted a study with different decision trees, but unlike Emel and Taşkın, they compared the performance of seven different methods instead of one method. In addition to all these studies, research conducted by the authors focusing on different methods of data mining are presented in more detail in the continuation of the chapter in order to show the different aspects of the methods and to prove their efficiency.

Over the years, the subject has started to become popular and the number of studies in the literature has increased. Thomas, Vinod and Raj (2014) aimed to classify spam documents by developing a computationally efficient classifier. Twelve feature selection techniques, namely TFDF, MI, PMI, NMI, CDM, WMI, Chi-square, NGL, GSS, CPD, Fisher Score and LTC, were applied and analyzed. As a result, it has been commented that RF with Symmetric Uncert FST model is better for classification of spam documents. Additionally, Guftar et al. (2015) aimed to present a new framework for estimating the possible causes of syncope. They were analyzed a dataset from Armed Forces Institute of Cardiology and the National Institute of Heart Disease (AFIC & NIHD from Rawalpindi, Pakistan, using RapidMiner. In conclusion, the proposed framework has been proven to improve prediction accuracy through the new clustering approach for possible causes of syncope. Data mining has continued to find its place in every field and has shown its productive side to everyone.

There are some other studies that focused on different situations. Naik and Samant (2016) classified 10 independent variables using liver patient data from Indian liver patients. In this chapter, in which a total of 583 samples were classified, Decision tree, Decision Stump, K-Nearest Neighbor and Naïve Bayes algorithms were used. They used the programs WEKA, Rapid miner, Tanagra, Orange and Knime. In the case of decision tree evaluation, the

Orange tool showed lower accuracy, while the Knime tool predicted better accuracy compared to its predecessor. And also, Wu et al. (2017) examined the purchasing behavior of more than 500,000 customers of the insurance company from China Life Insurance Company for 3 years. Researchers used SMOTE-based algorithms to analyze business data, in this way, they proposed the Random Forest algorithm using the parallel computing capability and memory caching mechanism optimized by Spark.

There are crises in the stock market that directly affect the economy. Therefore, it is very important to identify early warning indicators. Elagamy, Stanier and Sharp (2018) applied text mining and data mining applications to identify these critical indicators. Random Forest, Rotation Forest, Bagging, J48, Bayes Net, Decision table, Decision stump algorithms were used to classify the critical indicators of the stock market. The best performing algorithm was Random Forest algorithm. Random Forest, which was used in the classification of the dataset, provided 98.34% accuracy and correctly classified 535 of 544 articles. Likewise, Tan, Yan and Zhu (2019) aimed to predict the long-term and short-term price trend by using the data of the Chinese stock market between February 8, 2013 and August 8, 2017. In the same context, Livari and Ghalam (2020) aimed to group customers for a food manufacturing company using the variables of 2021 new purchases (R), frequency of purchases (F) and monetary value of purchase (M). By examining these variables, they used the K-Means algorithm and the Davies-Bouldin Index algorithms to cluster the customer group of the seedling production company. Customers were divided into three groups and marketing strategies were suggested on the basis of each group by calculating the customer lifetime value of each group.

In recent years, the number of studies has increased and data mining methods have become an important tool in predicting the future. Arminarahmah et al. (2021) aimed to view and map the spread of the COVID-19 virus in Asia with a dataset containing information on the basis of total cases, total deaths, total recovered and active cases from 2020, in 49 countries. They completed the research using data from the site such as WHO, CDC, NHC and worldometer. They used X-Means clustering method using RapidMiner. It was interpreted that the X-Means algorithm could be used to map the spread of COVID-19 in Asia, and it was divided into 4 regions according to the results of the spread mapping analysis. In different perspectives, there are some other studies conducted. Influencers promote their products using social media accounts such as Twitter, Facebook, and Instagram. Using the data collected from the marketing agency in Korea includes purchase information such as customer information, purchase item and payment amount from August 2018 to October 2020, Kim and Lee (2021) aimed to predict customer churn in influencer trading. They used the computer software program RapidMiner to predict lost customers. They achieved 90% accuracy by applying the Decision Tree algorithm. Also, Utomo (2021) aimed to analyze the data received from the Indonesian Ministry of Health on January 1, 2021 with using the clustering method. This chapter, which uses 2 attributes as confirmed and death cases, also includes information such as confirmed cases, treatment, recovery, and death cases. They compared the K-Means method with K-Medoids to cluster the spread of the coronavirus in Indonesia, as a result, it is seen that the best performing algorithm was the K-Means algorithm.

In addition, other studies carried out in 2021 can be summarized as following. Abdulkareem et al. (2021) aimed to observe the COVID-19 vaccine progress in the world by using machine learning classification algorithms. It has been discovered that the Decision Tree algorithm outperforms other algorithms in terms of accuracy and time criteria. In order to create sales clusters, Fithri and Wardhana (2021) aimed to analyze sales data with the support of the K-Means Clustering algorithm. As a result, 3 sales clusters were created, and it was suggested that sales cluster information could be an input for an alternative solution, inventory management and marketing strategies. Data clustering results from cluster1, cluster2 and cluster3 with 62%, 8%, and 30% percentage values, respectively. Evdokimova (2021) used segmentation (ABC and XYZ analysis) and clustering methods (K-means, X-means, Expectation-Maximization) in RapidMiner Studio to measure customer engagement. They processed large amounts of data to analyze their customer base. As a result, the best distribution of the customer base has been achieved by the Expectation-Maximization method.

Studies carried out in different sectors using different methods and software programs are presented in Table 1, and the algorithm with the best performance is highlighted as a result of the study. In this context, the studies summarized in the relevant table are shown on the basis of the author and year of publication, problem considered in the study, compared algorithms, algorithm that shows best performance, the accuracy of the algorithm and the software program used.

Table 1. Studies carried out in different sectors using different methods and software programs

Author(s)	Problem	Compared algorithms	Algorithm with best performance	Accuracy (%)	Program used
Haghanikha meneh et al. (2012)	Finding the highest performing tool	Naïve Bayes, Decision Tree, Support Vector Machine, K Nearest Neighbor, One Rule, Zero Rule	Decision Tree	97	Orange, Tanagra, KNIME, WEKA
Alsultanny (2013)	Forecasting the needs of the labor market	Naïve Bayes, Decision Tree, Decision Rules	Decision Tree	100	-
Thomas, Vinod, and Raj (2014)	Classify spam documents by developing a computationally efficient classifier	Naive Bayes, Random Forest, Random Tree, J48, Adaboosting	Random Forest	98,73	WEKA
Naik and Samant (2016)	Classifying people with and without liver	Decision Tree, Decision Stump, K-Nearest Neighbor, Naïve Bayes	K-Nearest Neighbor	99,70	WEKA, RapidMiner, Tanagra, Orange, Knime
Elagamy, Stanier, and Sharp (2018)	Classification of critical indicators of stock markets	Random Forest, Rotation Forest, Bagging, J48, Bayes Net, Decision Table, Decision Stump	Random Forest	98,34	-
Abdulkareem et al. (2021)	Observing COVID-19 vaccine progress around the world using machine learning classification algorithms	Decision Tree, K Nearest Neighbor, Random Forest, Naive Bayes	Decision Tree	99.9	WEKA

As a result, it has been observed that many studies in the literature are supported by different methods under the umbrella of data mining in many different fields. It has been observed that the studies have increased greatly in 2021, and that the methods under the umbrella of data mining are frequently examined by researchers and used to facilitate processes. In this direction, it has been determined that help is received from different software programs, but RapidMiner and WEKA are the programs that come to the fore the most.

Methodology

Decision trees, one of the tree-based learning algorithms, are the most used supervised learning algorithms. In general, they can be adapted to the solution of all the problems (classification and regression) considered. Therefore, it is very important for data analysts to learn and use these algorithms. The first cells of the decision trees are called the root or root node. Each observation is classified as "Yes" or "No" according to the root condition. Below the stem cells are interval nodes or nodes. Each observation is classified with the help of nodes. As the number of nodes increases, the complexity of the model also increases. At the bottom of the decision tree is the leaf nodes or leave. The leaves give us the result.

The Random Forest algorithm is a supervised classification algorithm. There are two stages in the Random Forest algorithm. The first of these stages is to create a Random Forest, and the other is to make predictions on the Random Forest classifier created in the first stage. The K-means algorithm provides an advantage in terms of being used in large data sets and providing ease of application. In this method, the number of clusters should be defined at the beginning, and it is not recommended to be used in categorical data sets. One of the disadvantages of the K-means algorithm is that it cannot give accurate results in data sets that differ in density and size. In addition, when factors such as unusual data and noise occur, k-means remains weak compared to other algorithms (Douzas, Bacao and Last, 2018). When using the K-means method, a local optimum point is calculated, and the method ends at this point (Ahmadyfard and Modares, 2008). Although the method is an iterative method, it aims to divide the square of the distance between the elements into the specified set using the minimization function. In each refresh, the data is sent to a different cluster and the optimum result is tried to be found. At this stage, a permutational operation is performed (Omran, Salman and Engelbrecht, 2006).

The X-means algorithm answers the question of how to find the number of k clusters by finding the optimum number. For this, it should be ensured that the number of K clusters is defined in a reasonable range. The number k in the specified range is scored by a model such as the Bayesian information criterion. In summary, it is examined from the lower limit to the upper limit of the determined range and works by adding a new center at the required point. The centroid with the best score among the k numbers scored in this process is considered optimum (Pelleg and Moore, 2000). The fact that the determined clustering algorithms have different features and processing methods, as stated above, is also included in the literature.

Cross Validation is used to evaluate the performance of predictive models and to prevent underfitting and overfitting when it comes to fit. Berrar (2018) performs performance measurement by separating the cross-validation dataset into two separate groups and using one of them as a training set and the other as a test set (Duda et al., 2005).

It also emphasized the importance of criteria while explaining the classification concept and formulation. It is not possible to think that one of the methods used in solving classification problems is better or worse than the other. At this point, it is necessary to act according to the suitability of the data set to the algorithm. There are established criteria to evaluate the performance of classification algorithms. At the beginning of these criteria, it can be defined as precision, Accuracy / Error Ratio, Specificity, Recall, F-measure, and ROC area. Confusion matrix is used to calculate the criteria. Shown as Confusion Matrix CMi,j, where i and j values are classes. CMi,j states that instances tagged in class j actually belong to class i. In the following example there is an example of a matrix with 2 different classes (Chandrashekar and Lee, 2019).

There are some terms and formulations used to interpret the outputs from data mining methods. Based on this in the software developed in the chapter, accuracy, sensitivity, and specificity values for classification problems are calculated with the formula given in Equations 1, 2 and 3, respectively.

$$Accuracy = \frac{TP + TN}{TP + FN + FP + TN} \quad (1)$$

$$Precision = \frac{TP}{TP + FP} \quad (2)$$

$$Specificity = \frac{TN}{TN + FN} \quad (3)$$

$$Accuracy\ Rate = \frac{(TP + TN)}{(TP + FN + FP + TN)} \quad (4)$$

$$Error\ Rate = \frac{(FN + FP)}{(FP + FN + FP + TN)} \quad (5)$$

True Positives (TP): These are instances where the true value is 1 and the predicted value is 1.

True Negatives (TN): These are instances where the true value is 0 and our predicted value is 0.

False Positives (FP): These are instances where the true value is 0 but the predicted value is 1.

False Negatives (FN): These are instances where the true value is 1 but our predicted value is 0.

It is desired to measure the true negative performance with the specificity criterion calculated in the third equation. It is the case that data that does not belong to class C are not defined in class C.

Precision refers to the ratio of positive samples classified in the correct category by the model to the total number of positive samples. In other words, it is the rate at which the data estimated as C is actually C. The precision measure measures the performance of the model in eliminating false positive data. The nominal value is the ratio of correctly classified samples belonging to the C class to the total C class. The rated measure measures the performance of eliminating false negative values, unlike the precision criterion.

$$\text{Recall} = \frac{TP}{TP + FN} \tag{6}$$

It is requested and expected that these two criteria give results close to 1.

The harmonic means of precision and recall measures is expressed as F and calculated as follows.

$$F = \frac{2 \times Precision \times Recall}{Precision + Recall} \tag{7}$$

When it is desired to be calculated by giving weight according to the precision criterion and the recall criterion, the F_b value is calculated as follows.

$$F_b = \frac{(1+b^2) \times Precision \times Recall}{b^2 \times Precision + Recall} \tag{8}$$

After calculating these values, the interpretation is more successful than the classifiers for which these values give larger results.

Findings and Results

Since 2019, the shopping habits of consumers have changed in accordance with the living conditions brought by the pandemic worldwide. Logistics/supply issues have gained importance with the concepts of online ordering and e-commerce. In this process, companies have directed business development studies, process shortening studies and activities to increase service quality in order to respond to demands faster by taking the road to be covered in a shorter time under normal conditions. The data set collected during the shopping of the customers of a business working in the retail sector and used in this chapter was created in August 2020 under pandemic conditions. In different time periods, in the take-away customer base, in addition to quantitative data such as age, gender, shopping unit, total amount, total weight, total shopping time, how many people are involved in the shopping; the information on which products they bought and the stability status of the customers from the moment they entered the store were examined. The related data set contains data in both string and integer formats. This data set, created with 213 customers and 16 different variables, allows working with almost all data mining methods. Using this data set, the intended solution is to determine the purchasing tendencies of customers with similar characteristics by looking at the characteristics of take-away customers given in the data set, and to achieve positive momentum that will affect the sales graph. Data mining studies are carried out using software specially developed for this subject, as the data is large-scale, as observed in the studies in the literature. SPSS, R, WEKA, Python, Orange, RapidMiner are the main ones. RapidMiner is an open-source program written in Java and can run on any operating system. In this chapter, it was preferred to use RapidMiner software by looking the last studies realized in this area because of its advantages.

The data set was tested with clustering and decision tree algorithms, in this way, the success rates of the algorithms on the data set were determined. First of all, the data set is run with various clustering algorithms, it is aimed to divide the customers into the most meaningful and most suitable clusters. Thus, various experiments were made, and it was seen that the distribution of the data was optimally distributed when k = 10 according to the characteristic of the data set. In Table 2, it was seen that the results of the two algorithms were close to each other, and a detailed examination was made. In Table 2, it has been determined which class the data clustered in the K-Means algorithm is included in the X-Means algorithm. For example, it has been seen that the data classified as cluster 2 in the K-Means algorithm are customers with id numbers corresponding to elements 8 of cluster 9 and element 5 of cluster 4 according to X-Means. In addition, according to K-Means, all elements of cluster 1 correspond to all elements of cluster 0 in X-Means. This proves that the two algorithms classify on the same basis at certain points. Based on all these, it can be interpreted that the two algorithms collect the data in similar groups.

Table 2. K-Means X-Means cluster comparison and classification equivalent of K-Means algorithm in X-Means algorithm

K means	X Means	K means	X Means
Cluster 0: 39 items	Cluster 0: 5 items	Cluster 0 (39)	Cluster 5 (39/45)
Cluster 1: 5 items	Cluster 1: 15 items	Cluster 1 (5)	Cluster 0 (5/5)
Cluster 2: 13 items	Cluster 2: 33 items	Cluster 2 (13)	Cluster9 (8/10), Cluster 4 (5/6)
Cluster 3: 17 items	Cluster 3: 6 items	Cluster 3 (17)	Cluster 1(15/15), Cluster 9 (2/9)
Cluster 4: 17 items	Cluster 4: 6 items	Cluster 4 (17)	Cluster 8 (17/38)
Cluster 5: 7 items	Cluster 5: 45 items	Cluster 5 (7)	Cluster 3 (6/6), Cluster 7 (53/53)
Cluster 6: 55 items	Cluster 6: 2 items	Cluster 6 (55)	Cluster 2(2/33), Cluster 7 (53/53)
Cluster 7: 2 items	Cluster 7: 53 items	Cluster 7 (2)	Cluster 7 (2/2)
Cluster 8: 27 items	Cluster 8: 38 items	Cluster 8 (27)	Cluster 5(6/45), Cluster 8 (21/38)
Cluster 9: 31 items	Cluster 9: 10 items	Cluster 9 (31)	Cluster 2 (31/33)
Total number of items: 213	Total number of items: 213	Total (213)	Total (213)

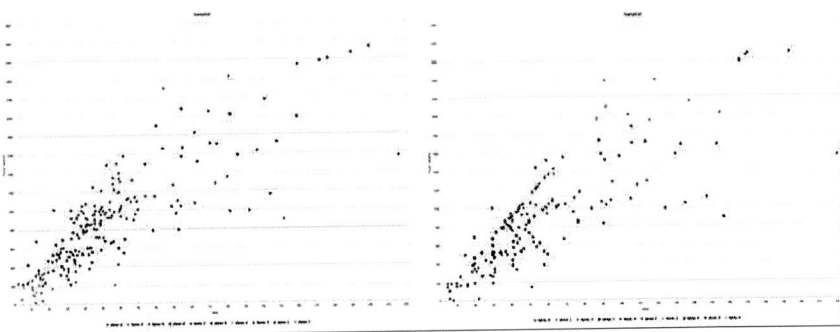

Figure 1. K-Means and X-Means dataset distribution.

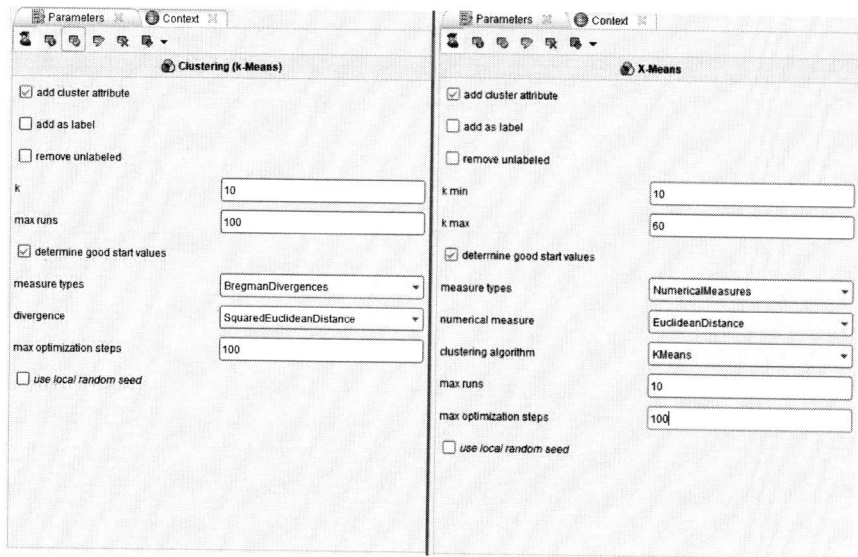

Figure 2. K-Means and X-Means parameters.

As can be seen in Table 2, as a result of the classification of the two algorithms, 205 out of 233 data are distributed in the same classes in the K-Means and X-Means algorithm. At this point, when a detailed examination was made, it was observed that the data classified in the K-Means algorithm was included in the X-Means algorithm, as in Table 2, and it was observed that even though the names of the classes were changed, it was still in the same class with 88% probability. In Figure 1, point graphs of these classifications are given. When examined visually, the data distribution supports the results in Table 2. Despite the 14 features in the data set, it has been determined that the operators in the RapidMiner program give lower priority when the clustering algorithms are applied, while some parameters stand out according to their weights to the result. These parameters, which have a low effect on the result, were neglected in the classification process, instead of all 14 features, the chapter was carried out on the parameters seen in Figure 2. The methods used in clustering analysis process data based on similar distances. Methods such as Standardized Euclidean, Square Euclidean, Euclidean, Canberra, Manhattan Mahalanobis, Minkowski can be used to determine these distances. Since each method has a different technique, it is necessary to be careful in the application of cluster analysis. As seen in Figure 1, the basis of the clustering algorithm is that each element has similar characteristics with the other elements in its own group and it has features that distinguish the groups from each other. The K-Means algorithm provides an advantage in terms of being used in large data sets and providing ease of application. In this method, the number of clusters must be defined initially. When using the K-Means method, a local optimum point is calculated, and the method ends at this point. Although the method is an iterative method, it aims to divide the square of the distance between the elements into the specified set using the minimization function. In each refresh, the data is sent to a different cluster and the optimum result is tried to be found. At this stage, a permutational operation is performed.

The X-Means algorithm answers the question of how to find the number of k clusters by finding th optimum number. For this, it should be ensured that the number of k clusters is defined in a reasonable range. The number k in the specified range is scored by a model such as the Bayesian information criterion. In summary, this algorithm works by examining from the lower limit to the upper limit of the determined range and adding a new center at the required point. The centroid with the best score among the k numbers scored in this process is considered optimum. The determined clustering algorithms have different features and processing methods within themselves. The resulting methodological differences as shown in Figure 1 directly affect the results and cause the data to be divided into different classes. Figure 2 shows the parameters used for the K-Means and X-Means algorithms.

Clusters in the results of the K-Means algorithm, one of the clustering methods, were included in the data set and studied with the help of Decision Tree and Random Forest, which are Decision Tree methods, and supported by Cross Validation due to the small amount of data. Cross Validation is used to evaluate the performance of predictive models and to prevent underfitting and overfitting when it comes to fit (Berrar, 2018). Cross-validation divides the data set into two separate groups and uses one of them as a training set and the other as a test set and performs performance measurement (Duda et al., 2005).

There are established criteria to evaluate the performance of classification algorithms. At the beginning of these criteria are precision, accuracy / error rate, specificity, recall, F-measure, and ROC area. Confusion matrix is used to calculate the criteria. Confusion Matrix is denoted as $CM_{i,j}$ where i and j values are classes. $CM_{i,j}$ indicates that the instances tagged in class j actually belong to class i. In the following example there is an example of a matrix with 2 different classes.

As can be seen in Table 3, the matrix is divided into 4 areas, and the values of these areas are determined according to whether the data is classified correctly or incorrectly. Field A is named as true positive, and it means that the data of the C_1 class in the training set is defined as C_1 again. (B field false negative) Represents data that is not defined as C_1 in the test set, although it is in the C_1 class in the training set. The C false positive area is the area not defined as C_1 but classified as C_1 when estimating. The D negative field is the field that is not in the C_1 class and is not predicted as C_1. By using these values, calculations related to accuracy and error rate were made.

In Table 4 and Figure 3, the estimation performances of the model applied on the test data are given. In Figure 3, correctly predicted data are marked in orange and incorrect ones in gray. Class precision and class recall values in row and column subtotals are given in Table 3. From these values, with class precision, the correct classification percentage of the Decision Tree algorithm is calculated as 81.13% and the average of Recall values is 71.70%. In the Random Forest algorithm, the percentage of correct classification is 85.71% and the average of Recall values is 88.33%. As can be understood from here, the Random Forest model performed better in estimation than the Decision Tree model.

Table 3. The structure of the confusion matrix

		Predicted Values	
		Positive (C_1)	Negative ($-C_1$)
Actual Values	Positive (C_1)	A: True Positive (TP)	B: False Negative (FN)
	Negative ($-C_1$)	C: False Positive (FP)	D: True Negative (TN)

Table 4. Comparison of the success rate of algorithms

Decision Tree	Class precision average	81.13%
	Class Recall average	71.70%
Random Forest	Class precision average	85.71%
	Class Recall average	88.33%

When choosing the CART algorithm to distribute the model in the Decision Tree model, all the predicted values are the same, which means that this model has poor performance. Instead of creating a single tree, the Random Forest model creates several trees that branch out all the nodes based on the best of the randomly picked features at each node.

Datasets are produced as a result of the displacement of the data in the dataset. No pruning is done, and random trees are developed. In decision trees, a node represents the entire instance because it is the test performed for a feature. The branch represents the result of the test performed, and the leaves represent the classes as undivided nodes. The root node is the top node and it is a model that works from top to bottom.

Accuracy: 83.59%	True cluster_8	True cluster_1	True cluster_7	True cluster_5	True cluster_9	True cluster_2	True cluster_3	True cluster_4	True cluster_0	True cluster_6	Class precision
Pred cluster_8	37	0	0	2	0	0	0	0	0	0	94.87%
Pred cluster_1	0	8	0	0	3	0	0	0	0	0	72.73%
Pred cluster_7	0	7	50	0	2	6	0	1	0	0	75.76%
Pred cluster_5	1	0	1	43	0	4	0	0	0	0	87.76%
Pred cluster_9	0	0	0	0	4	0	0	2	0	0	66.67%
Pred cluster_2	0	0	2	0	0	23	0	0	0	0	92.00%
Pred cluster_3	0	0	0	0	0	0	5	1	0	1	71.43%
Pred cluster_4	0	0	0	0	0	0	1	2	0	0	66.67%
Pred cluster_0	0	0	0	0	1	0	0	0	5	0	83.33%
Pred cluster_6	0	0	0	0	0	0	0	0	0	1	100.00%
Class Recall	97.37%	53.33%	94.34%	95.56%	92.00%	69.70%	83.33%	33.33%	100.00%	50.00%	

Accuracy: 98.59%	True cluster_8	True cluster_1	True cluster_7	True cluster_5	True cluster_9	True cluster_2	True cluster_3	True cluster_4	True cluster_0	True cluster_6	Class precision
Pred cluster_8	37	0	0	0	0	0	0	0	0	0	100.00%
Pred cluster_1	0	15	0	0	0	0	0	0	0	0	100.00%
Pred cluster_7	0	0	53	0	0	0	0	0	0	0	100.00%
Pred cluster_5	0	0	0	45	0	0	0	0	0	0	100.00%
Pred cluster_9	0	0	0	0	30	0	0	0	0	0	100.00%
Pred cluster_2	0	0	0	0	0	33	0	0	0	0	100.00%
Pred cluster_3	0	0	0	0	0	0	6	1	0	0	85.71%
Pred cluster_4	0	0	0	0	0	0	0	5	0	0	100.00%
Pred cluster_0	0	0	0	0	0	0	0	0	5	2	71.43%
Pred cluster_6	0	0	0	0	0	0	0	0	0	0	0.00%
Class Recall	100.00%	100.00%	100.00%	100.00%	100.00%	100.00%	100.00%	100.00%	100.00%	100.00%	

Figure 3. Decision Tree and Random Forest output.

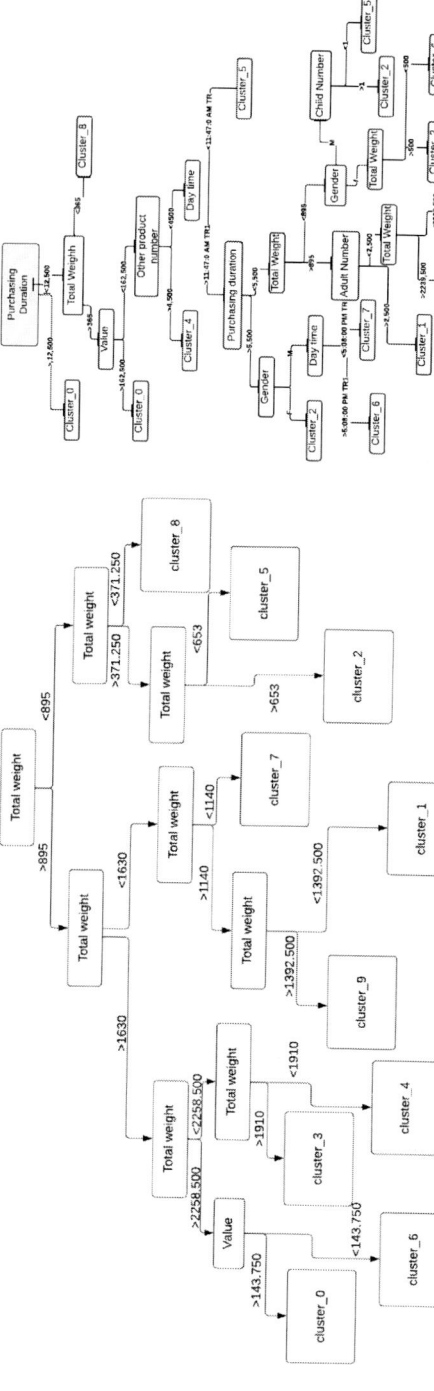

Figure 4. Decision Tree obtained by Decision Tree algorithm and Random Forest.

With the Decision Tree, we see that the first node is separated according to the total weight, while in the Random Forest method, we see that the first node is the purchase time. Images of decision trees obtained by Decision Tree and Random Forest algorithms are given in Figure 4. Although the Random Forest model, from the way it is expressed with colors under the clusters in the images, performs better in estimating, it is seen that the criterion of the homogeneity of the subset in the decision trees stands out more in the Decision Tree. As a result, with all these findings, it was seen that the Random Forest algorithm performed more successfully than the Decision Tree algorithm in the analysis on the data set processed and specified in the RapidMiner program.

Conclusion

Since 2019, consumers' shopping habits have changed due to limited living conditions around the world. The data set used in this chapter consists of data collected under pandemic conditions in August 2020. The aim was to form a basis for the online shopping activities of retail businesses under pandemic conditions. By examining the local customer base and assuming that the same customer group will exhibit similar behaviors in online or tele-ordering methods, it was desired to work on customer identification and order estimation in order to follow an effective sales policy.

At the beginning of the chapter, first of all, clustering algorithms were used for customer segmentation, and it was aimed to group the customers with similar characteristics. Thus, it is aimed to reach the result in a shorter time by including the customers with certain characteristics, rather than each customer being a value on its own.

In order to make predictions on the customers divided into clusters, decision tree algorithms were tried, and it was investigated which algorithm would perform higher in the relevant data set. The aim here was to develop effective sales strategies by looking at the branches of the algorithm with the highest performance.

The effect of the existing differences in the functioning of the selected methods on the result was observed, and the reasons for which method was appropriate were investigated. At this point, the output of the chapter is an exemplary chapter, in addition to the existing information in the literature, in terms of reference to studies that will be compared in performance on similar data sets in which integer and string values are handled in a mixed manner.

As stated in the findings section, the randomness of the Random Forest model and the creation of multiple trees in the chapter created a positive value, resulting in a higher performance than the Decision Tree method, which works on estimating a single tree and the same data.

In order to make additional predictions to the algorithms studied for the future, the effectiveness of models such as Chadi, ID3, logistic regression, gradient boosted tree can be tested, and comparisons can be made. It will help to determine the most suitable estimation model for the data set by investigating the causality in the performance differences. At the same time, causality can be investigated by observing the differences between the coding-based programs and the programs working with the help of operators by means of WEKA, SPSS, R language, Python, Orange, which are used in data mining studies.

References

Abdulkareem, N. M., Abdulazeez, A. M., Zeebaree, D. Q., and Hasan, D. A. (2021). COVID-19 World Vaccination Progress Using Machine Learning Classification Algorithms. *Qubahan Academic Journal*, 1 (2), 100–105.

Ahmadyfard, A., and Modares, H. (2008). Combining PSO and K-Means to Enhance Data Clustering. *2008 International Symposium on Telecommunications*, IST 2008, 688–691.

Alsultanny, Y. A. (2013). Labor Market Forecasting by Using Data Mining. *Procedia Computer Science*, 18, 1700–1709.

Arminarahmah, N., Daengs, A., Bhawika, G. W., Dewi, M. P., and Wanto, A. (2021). Mapping the Spread of Covid-19 in Asia Using Data Mining X-Means Algorithms. *IOP Conference Series: Materials Science and Engineering*, 1071 (1), 012018.

Balabantaray, R. C., Sarma, C., and Jha, M. (2015). *Document Clustering Using K-Means and K-Medoids*. http://arxiv.org/abs/1502.07938.

Berrar, D. (2018). Cross-Validation. *Encyclopedia of Bioinformatics and Computational Biology: ABC of Bioinformatics*, 1–3, 542–545.

Chandrashekar, M., and Lee, Y. (2019). MCDD: Multi-Class Distribution Model for Large Scale Classification. *Proceedings - 2018 IEEE International Conference on Big Data, Big Data*, 2018, 4906–4914.

Douzas, G., Bacao F., and Last, F. (2018). Improving Imbalanced Learning through a Heuristic Oversampling Method Based on K-Means and SMOTE. *Information Sciences*, 465, 1–20.

Duda, S., Miller, A. R., Statnikov, A., and Johnson, K. (2005). Extracting Drug-Drug Interaction Articles from MEDLINE to Improve the Content of Drug Databases. *AMIA Annual Symposium Proceedings/AMIA Symposium. AMIA Symposium*, 216–220.

Elagamy, M. N., Stanier, C., and Sharp, B. (2018). Stock Market Random Forest-Text Mining System Mining Critical Indicators of Stock Market Movements. *2nd International Conference on Natural Language and Speech Processing*, ICNLSP 2018, 1–8.

Emel, G. G., and Taşkın, Ç. (2005). Veri Madenciliğinde Karar Ağaçları ve Bir Satış Analizi Uygulaması [*Decision Trees in Data Mining and a Sales Analysis Application*], 6 (2), 221–239.

Evdokimova, S. A. (2021). Segmentation of Store Customers to Increase Sales Using ABC-XYZ-Analysis and Clustering Methods. *Journal of Physics, Conference Series*, 2032 (1).

Fithri, F. A., and Wardhana, S. (2021). Cluster Analysis of Sales Transaction Data Using K-Means Clustering At Toko Usaha Mandiri. *Jurnal PILAR Nusa Mandiri*, 17 (2), 113–118.

Garcia, C. D. S., Meincheim, A., Junior, E. R. F., Dallagassa, M. R., Sato, D. M. V., Carvalho, D. R., Santos, E. A. P., and Scalabrin, E. E. (2019). Process Mining Techniques and Applications – A Systematic Mapping Study. *Expert Systems with Applications*, 133, 260–295.

Gibert, K., Izquierdo, J., Sànchez-Marrè, M., Hamilton, S. H., Rodríguez-Roda, I., and Holmes, G. (2018). Which Method to Use? An Assessment of Data Mining Methods in Environmental Data Science. *Environmental Modelling and Software*, 110, 3–27.

Guftar, M., Ali, S. H., Raja, A. A., and Qamar, U., (2015). A Novel Framework for Classification of Syncope Disease Using K-Means Clustering Algorithm. *IntelliSys 2015 - Proceedings of 2015 SAI Intelligent Systems Conference*, 127–132.

Haghanikhameneh, F., Panahy, P. H. S., Khanahmadliravi, N., and Mousavi, S. A. (2012). A Comparison Study between Data Mining Algorithms over Classification Techniques in Squid Dataset. *International Journal of Artificial Intelligence*, 9 (12 A), 59–66.

Kale, B., and Yüksel, G., (2020). Veri Madenciliği Sınıflandırma Algoritmaları Ile E-Posta Önemliliğinin Belirlenmesi. *Ç.Ü Fen ve Mühendislik Bilimleri Dergisi* [Determination of E-Mail Importance with Data Mining Classification Algorithms. *CU Journal of Science and Engineering Sciences*], 39 (9).

Kim, S., and Lee, H. (2021). Customer Churn Prediction in Influencer Commerce: An Application of Decision Trees. *Procedia Computer Science*, 199, 1332–1339.

Larson, D., and Chang, V. (2016). A Review and Future Direction of Agile, Business Intelligence, Analytics and Data Science. *International Journal of Information Management*, 36 (5), 700–710.

Livari, R. T. and Ghalam, N. Z. (2020). Customers Grouping Using Data Mining Techniques in the Food Distribution Industry (A Case Study). *SRPH Journal of Applied Management and Agile Organisation*.

Naik, A., and Samant, L. (2016). Correlation Review of Classification Algorithm Using Data Mining Tool: WEKA, Rapidminer, Tanagra, Orange and Knime. *Procedia Computer Science*, 85, 662–668.

Omran, M. G. H., Salman, A., and Engelbrecht, A. P. (2006). Dynamic Clustering Using Particle Swarm Optimization with Application in Image Segmentation. *Pattern Analysis and Applications*, 8 (4), 332–344.

Pelleg, D., and Moore, A. (2000). X-Means: Extending K-Means with Efficient Estimation of the Number of Clusters. *ICML '00: Proceedings of the Seventeenth International Conference on Machine Learning.*

Tan, Y., Chen, H., Zhang, J., Tang, R., and Liu, P. (2022). Early Risk Prediction of Diabetes Based on GA-Stacking. *Applied Sciences (Switzerland),* 12 (2).

Tan, Z., Yan, Z., and Zhu, G. (2019). Stock Selection with Random Forest: An Exploitation of Excess Return in the Chinese Stock Market. *Heliyon,* 5 (8), e02310.

Thomas, J. P. V., and Raj, N. S. (2014). Towards Spam Mail Detection Using Robust Feature Evaluated with Feature Selection Techniques. *International Journal of Engineering and Technology,* 6 (5), 2144–2158.

Utomo, W. (2021). The Comparison of K-Means and k-Medoids Algorithms for Clustering the Spread of the Covid-19 Outbreak in Indonesia. *ILKOM Jurnal Ilmiah,* 13 (1), 31–35.

Wei, C. P., and Chiu, I. T. (2002). Turning Telecommunications Call Details to Churn Prediction: A Data Mining Approach. *Expert Systems with Applications,* 23 (2), 103–112.

Wu, Z., Lin, W., Zhang, Z., Wen, A., and Lin, L. (2017). An Ensemble Random Forest Algorithm for Insurance Big Data Analysis. *Proceedings - 2017 IEEE International Conference on Computational Science and Engineering and IEEE/IFIP International Conference on Embedded and Ubiquitous Computing, CSE and EUC 2017,* 1, 531–36.

Chapter 4

Analysis of Customer Churn in the Banking Industry Using Data Mining

Özge Doğuç[*]
Management Information Systems, Medipol University,
Istanbul, Turkey

Abstract

Today, banks have a very important place in the great economic environments of countries. As in every sector, there are many competitors and a great competitive environment in the banking field. Especially individual customers prefer digital channels to make their banking transactions faster and easier. Banks need to take fast and industry-leading steps to meet these expectations of their customers. They need to differentiate themselves from the competition with innovative features by giving importance to digital. The main goals of the banks in the competitive environment are gaining new customers, increasing customer loyalty, reducing customer churn rates, and providing superior customer satisfaction. In this study, customer data belonging to a bank were analyzed with data analysis algorithms. Customer churn analysis was performed using different machine algorithms. The model was created on the Knime platform. This study performs a customer loss analysis using data mining algorithms. The aim is to reveal the reasons for losing customers, the elements of customer loyalty and to help develop customer relations activities accordingly.

Keywords: customer relations, customer loyalty, churn customers, data analysis

---

[*] Corresponding Author's Email: odoguc@medipol.edu.tr.

In: The Future of Data Mining
Editor: Cem Ufuk Baytar
ISBN: 979-8-88697-250-4
© 2022 Nova Science Publishers, Inc.

Introduction

Companies attach importance to customer loyalty in an increasingly competitive environment. Acquiring new customers is more costly than increasing the loyalty of an existing customer and keeping them from leaving.

Systems that predict customers who are likely to abandon will contribute to marketing and customer loyalty efforts. By focusing on this customer group, companies can solve the customer loss problem. In this study, it is aimed to analyze customer churn by using three data mining algorithms.

Knime and Python are used in this study. Knime is an open source and multiplatform software data analysis, reporting and integrating platform. It is used in pharmaceutical research and analysis in the fields of CRM, business intelligence and finance. In this study, it was used in the stages of understanding the data and creating a model. Python language is a widely used software language in the field of data mining. NumPy, SciPy, MatPlotLib, SciKit-Learn, Pandas libraries are data mining libraries used for data visualization, processing, regression and many more analysis. In this study, the Python language was used in the stages of understanding, interpreting, and visualizing the data set.

In this study, customer loss estimation was made by using Decision Tree and Random Forest algorithms, which are classification techniques of supervised learning algorithms, and Artificial Neural Network. The accuracy of the models was found, and the models were compared. The accuracy values of all three models were close to each other. The Random Forest algorithm caught the highest value with 0.864. The current data set has been obtained from a publicly available source on the internet. The value of the target (class) variable in the data set we are trying to predict, the value of the customer leaving is 1, and the equivalent of not leaving is 0. There was a number imbalance between the two values in the data set. Therefore, data increase has been achieved by using the SMOTE node. Thus, an increase in the accuracy value was observed. For the algorithms to have the best success values, experiments were made by giving different values to the hyperparameters we gave. The data mining methodology, CRIPS-DM (Cross-Industry Standard Process for Data Mining), has been followed. Understanding the problem and data; cleaning the data, making it usable; The stages of modeling and model evaluation and comparison of success values have been completed. A roadmap was drawn for the final implementation phase.

Digitalization and Online Banking

Definitions of digitization vary. Sassen (Sassen, 2000) stated that in terms of economy, digitalization expands the borders of the country, thereby increasing convenience and globalization. He stated that with the digitalization of the economy and globalization, later on, concepts such as sovereignty, culture and capital were affected. Today, digitalization has experienced changes for both companies and societies and continues to be up-to-date. New technologies have been adopted within the company, causing significant changes. The study of Parviainen et al. (Parviainen et al., 2017) has set a right starting point and presented a model that aims to help companies to incorporate digital transformation in a systematic way. The stages of the company's implementation of the roadmap in order to reach the targets, after the digitalization positioning, determination of the targets, analysis of the current digital situation, were conveyed to the companies. Although this process differs for each company, the work of Parviainen et al. has provided guidance on the steps companies should take in their digitalization journey (Parviainen et al., 2017).

Digitalization has brought different approaches in the services provided to customers by each sector. The relationship established with the customer in banking was renewed. The bank's digital information systems operation had to reach the customer through the transfer of branch personnel. With the online banking interfaces, the banking transaction limits of the customers are self-determined and spread to all possible places. The products of the banks have turned into providing information technology services directly to the customers by leaving the service they provide only in their branches. Online banking has made it possible for the customer to access account and transaction information, create orders, requests, and perform many services directly at any time, such as money transfer according to needs (Gupta and Kamilla, 2014).

Apart from cash withdrawal, internet banking allows customers to easily perform all kinds of transactions. As people's lives get more intense, their demands for products that are easier and more widely used have increased. Using information technologies has gained importance to increase customer loyalty and product usage. A customer's perceived trust in online banking services is one of the factors affecting the customer's loyalty to the bank and the degree of adoption. The level of trust the bank establishes with the customer through the technological interface affects the customer's future commitment to online banking (Mukherjee and Nath, 2003).

Customer Relations Management and Data Analysis

Customer relationship management has become an area that benefits from and is fed by data mining analysis due to the increasing technology, competitive environment, and information age. Customer relationship management aims to increase customer loyalty, to be in constant communication with the customer and to provide the right service at the right time. These positive relations with the customer are important in terms of reducing customer loss rates and acquiring new customers in the company's competitive environment. Using information systems and algorithms to make sound decisions about the future will bring significant advances in all areas of the company (Payne, 2005).

As a result of today's technological developments, increasing data collection and storage possibilities, producing meaningful information from these data has become one of the issues that companies attach importance to. The usage methods of this data may vary in each sector. The problem to be solved, the data used, the algorithms used may be different for each company and sector. The study by Doğan et al. (Doğan, Erol and Buldu, 2014) includes the use of data analysis algorithms in terms of customer relationship management in the insurance industry. This study belongs to the various insurance policy sales made by one of the most important insurance companies in Turkey between 2010 and 2012. The data consists of approximately 12 thousand lines and 9 columns containing various insurance information such as motor insurance, fire, earthquake. To ensure personal information security, the customer ID and number are hidden. Apriori algorithm was used. The letters "T and F" are used to represent whether there is a fuse or not. After the data pre-preparation, the analysis phase was started. The association was analyzed, and significant results were revealed such as "47% of those who purchased compulsory earthquake insurance also bought fire insurance." In the light of this information, it will be possible to organize campaigns that will attract the attention of the customer in future campaigns. In the insurance sector, it is possible to obtain meaningful information through data analysis by using customer data and to use this information in customer relationship management and marketing activities. As a result of this study, it has been shown that by looking at the preferred policy types, strategies such as which customer will be directed to which campaign in the future, and thus efficiency can be increased.

Hsieh's study (Hsieh, 2004) includes analyzing bank customer data with data mining and drawing conclusions. The databases are large as banks have daily and monthly transaction surpluses, registered accounts and a wide range of customers. Data analysis studies are also challenging. This study was also conducted on credit card customers and a behavioral scoring model was created by analyzing the historical data of existing customers. Three main profitable customer groups were separated by using variables such as repayment behavior, frequency of use, duration of use and demographic information. Apriori association algorithm was used. This study shows that identifying customers with the behavioral scoring model provides useful information and facilitates marketing strategy development. As a result, it has been shown that credit and behavior scoring models are useful and this study will be useful in making a more accurate decision on whether to give credit to newly made loan applicants. It helped marketers determine efficient strategies with customer profiles and conduct more personalized marketing customer relations.

Gürsoy's (Gürsoy, 2010) study titled "Customer Dropout Analysis in the Telecommunication Sector" studied churn customer loss with data analysis algorithms in the telecommunication sector. If a customer cancels their membership agreement with a company and becomes a customer of another competitor, that customer is called a lost customer or a Churn customer. Loss of customers is closely related to customer loyalty. Price advantages are not enough to keep the customer. Adding new value-added services to products is an important point to ensure customer loyalty. The main purpose of customer churn analysis is to find a customer that is likely to be lost and to take marketing or other strategic steps to avoid losing those customers. The lost customers to be considered in the analysis differ according to the sectors or data. For example, a credit card customer can easily start using another bank's credit card without canceling the current bank's credit card. In this case, one can look at the rate of reduction in expenses to understand the loss of the customer. Loss of customers can be a big problem in competitive banks, insurance, and telecommunications companies. The cost of acquiring new customers for companies is increasing day by day. Instead of organizing campaigns to gain new customers, companies care about higher customer loyalty. Having a good model that handles large amounts of data will help companies to plan competitive advantage and more accurate strategies. In the study of Şimşek and Oman (Şimşek, 2018), customer loss estimation of a telecommunication company in Turkey was made with SPSS. Identifying which customers are likely to lose, determining which customers should retain, and developing strategies to retain profitable customers are matters of customer retention. Firstly, it is very important to determine the churn ratio.

By using this ratio, companies can make predictions about the future behavior of new customers and develop appropriate strategies beforehand.

Logistic regression and decision tree algorithms were used in this study. The target variable in the data set, customer leaving and not leaving, is given as 0, 1. After preprocessing the data, the split ratios of 0 and 1 were balanced as 49% to 50%. The next step is to eliminate variables that have no effect on the target variable. By examining the correlation between the variables, the determined variables are eliminated. As a result of the decision tree model, meaningful information such as "If the average of local and long-distance calls is higher than 218, 42% of the subscribers will go to churn" was obtained. The prediction accuracy rate of the logistic regression model that they did not churn was 74%, and the accuracy rate of prediction that they did not churn was 66%. As a result, the information obtained from this study can be used in marketing activities. When campaigns are organized for products and services, it can prioritize subscribers who are more likely to churn, thus reducing customer churn (Gürsoy, 2010).

The study by Savaşçı and Tatlıdil (Savaşçı and Tatlıdil, 2006) includes the evaluation of the practices of banks in customer relations in terms of customer loyalty. Banks in the financial services sector aim to increase customer loyalty, maintain the number of customers, and ensure satisfaction by giving importance to customer relations. A customer data warehouse needs to be created. In this study, customer impression is provided through credit cards. Credit card strategies used for customer loyalty were evaluated. A survey method was determined for 500 card users in İzmir district. The reasons for using the most preferred credit cards by the consumers participating in the survey were examined. When asked whether they use the installment facility with their credit cards, 91% stated that they pay their purchases in installments. The advantage with the highest level of satisfaction of the card(s) they use the most is that it is wide and easy to use at a rate of 84%. Banks attach great importance to customer relationship management to retain their customers and increase customer loyalty and satisfaction in today's technology and competitive environment. For this, it is important to keep customer data, to obtain meaningful results by using data mining methods, and to use communication technologies effectively and efficiently.

In the study of Gülpınar (Gülpinar, 2013), estimating customer loss in the Turkish telecommunications sector with Artificial Neural Network analysis and considering incoming outgoing calls, because of Social Network analysis, it shows appropriate marketing activities for effective customers. A 14-question survey was conducted with 100 different GSM users. For the Social

Network analysis, the phone numbers of the 5 people they talked to last time were asked and a survey was conducted with them. Thus, a wide communication network was created. A high iteration model was created, and the margin of error was reduced below 0.05. This study has added a different approach to customer loss analysis by examining the communication network structures of customers using social network analysis. What influences customer value is not only their own behavior, but also the customer's network. In the telecommunication sector, besides his personal characteristics, the people he is connected to have affected the loss of customers. In other fields such as banking, this approach to customer analysis will support the emergence of better forecasting methods.

In a competitive telecommunications market, the company's goal of minimizing customer loss by increasing customer loyalty is as important as gaining customers. As studies have shown, spending on acquiring customers is 20 times more costly than retaining existing customers. Customer relationship management (CRM) establishes and manages strong, long-term customer relationships with high loyalty. For this purpose, customer loss analysis tools are developed and benefited from. (Vafeiadis et al., 2015)

Customer Loyalty and Data Analysis

It is important for companies to be able to estimate the amount of revenue they can generate from their active customers. Therefore, companies need models that will determine whether their customers are loyal to the company or not and determine the number of customers who will leave the company and turn to their competitors. The cost of acquiring a new customer is often higher than the cost of retaining a customer. These models are especially important for the modern telecommunication operator. In the study of Wijaya and Girsang (Wijaya and Girsang, 2015), C4.5, Naive Bayes and Nearest Neighbor Algorithms and data mining estimation of the national multimedia company in Indonesia were studied. As a result, modeling customer loyalty degrees with mathematical methods is beneficial for companies. These models will help the company better forecast its revenues. With the development of database and computing technology, data collection and storage processes have become easier and faster. Thus, data mining processes increase and allow us to obtain models with high success rates. The C4.5 algorithm was the algorithm with the highest accuracy.

The study of Ivanchenko et al. (Ivanchenko et al., 2019) on developing a marketing relationship based on data mining in the banking sector will help the sector in catching the advantages and opportunities in this field. This study shows data mining methods and successful examples of Russian banks in this field. It gives advice on the use of data mining in determining digital marketing banking strategies. A Russian bank uses big data analytics to manage risks, fight fraud, segment customers and evaluate customers' credit ratings, manage personnel, segment customer churn, create financial statements, and analyze posts on social networks and forums. The positive effects of providing personalized offers based on outputs from data analysis for customers through the Call Center have emerged. Contributions of using data analysis technologies; individual customer satisfaction, service planning according to customer needs, increase in customer loyalty and attracting the right target customer with low costs.

The study by Maryani et al. (Maryani and Riana, 2017) aims to perform clustering and customer profiling for mid-industry companies using the Recency Frequency and Monetary (RFM) model for customer relationship management. Customer segmentation, classification and determination of customer loyalty levels were carried out with K-means and decision tree algorithms.

Tools and Methodology

In this study, Decision Tree, Random Forest, and Artificial Neural Networks data mining algorithms were applied on a data set containing bank customer data. Data mining methodology, which stands for CRIPS-DM, is Cross-Industry Standard Process for Data Mining. This is the most widely used model in data mining and data science and has 6 stages.

- Business Understanding: It is the stage where the goals and needs of the business are understood.
- Data Understanding: It is the stage of understanding the data. It starts with data collection. It is the stage of understanding the data and forming the first impression.
- Data Preparation: It is the stage of organizing the data set that we have scattered in accordance with the model we will establish. Operations

such as selecting data variables, cleaning data, placing missing data, data type conversion can be done.
- Modeling: It is the stage of choosing various data mining algorithms that we will apply to the data we have prepared, determining the parameters, and applying the model.
- Evaluation: It is the stage of finding the evaluation scores of the model such as accuracy and sensitivity by comparing the target variable assumptions of the established model, which we call class, with the test data. As a result of these trials, the model is reviewed, and improvements are made if necessary.
- Implementation: It is the final stage. The model is presented to the necessary users and brought to life in a way that it will be used in accordance with its purpose (Alaybeg, 2019).

In this study, the data set consisting of 10,000 customers obtained from open sources for customer churn analysis includes 14 variables. One of them is the exit (Exited) target (class) variable that is tried to be estimated. These are the variables;

- Registration id (RowNumber), Customer number (CustomerId), Customer surname (Surname): These are the variables that have no effect on the customer's departure from the bank. They did not participate in modelling.
- Credit score (CreditScore): A customer with a high credit score is less likely to leave the bank, which can have an impact on customer churn.
- Geography: customer location can have an impact on customer churn.
- Gender: It may be necessary to examine the effects on customer churn.
- Age (Age): It influences the loss of customers. Older and younger customers may have different behaviors.
- Usage period (Tenure): Refers to the number of years the customer has been a customer of the bank.
- Balance: It is the customer's account balance amount, it influences customer loss.
- Number of products (NumOfProducts): It is the number of products purchased by the customer through the bank.
- Credit card ownership (HasCrCard): Indicates whether the customer has a credit card. (0 as 1)

- Activity (IsActiveMember): Indicates the customer's activity according to the number of transactions. (in 0.1)
- Estimated Salary: People with low salaries may be more likely to leave the bank than people with high salaries. It is a continuous numeric variable.
- Lost (Exited): The bank customer's exit status is the target (class) variable. (0: didn't leave, 1: left)

Understanding the Data

After understanding the purpose of the first stage of the CRIPS-DM methodology, the stage of understanding the data was started. At this stage, the Python programming language was used. The dataset was read, and tables were extracted using the Seaborn and Matplotlib.pyplot libraries for statistical graphs. Pandas, numpy library was used and data preliminary information was obtained with appropriate codes. This phase has been completed by using some nodes in Knime.

Table 1. Variable properties of age and credit score

	Age (Age)	Credit Score
Number (Count)	1000.000000	1000.000000
Average (Mean)	38,921800	650.528800
Standard deviation (std)	10.487806	96.653299
Min value	18,000,000	350,000,000
First 25% average	32,000,000	584,000,000
First 50% average	37,000,000	652,000,000
First 75% average	44,000,000	718,000,000
Max value	92,000,000	850,000,000
Graphic		
explanation	It is seen that the extreme data is after the age of 60.	It is seen that the extreme data is before 400.

Table 2. Variable properties of number of products and estimated salary

	Number of Products (Num of Products)	Estimated Salary
Number (Count)	1000.000000	1000.000000
Average (Mean)	1.530200	100090.239881
Standard deviation (std)	0.581654	57510.492818
Min value	1.000000	11.580000
Average of the first 25%	1.000000	51002.110000
Average of the first 50%	1.000000	100193.915000
Average of the first 75%	2,000,000	149388.247500
Max value	4,000,000	199992.480000
Graphic		
explanation	There is a total of 60 people with 4 product ownership, seen as extreme data. 1 and 2 have agglomeration.	It is seen that the estimated salary distribution is balanced.

The characteristics of the variables of Age, Credit Score, Number of Products and Estimated Salary in the data set are given in Table 1 and Table 2.

The correlation relationship between the variables was examined. If there were variables with a correlation ratio greater than 0.5, we would have taken it into account. The highest values are between 0.3 on the negative side and Balance and NumOfProducts. The correlation graph is given in Figure 1.

Correlation coefficients were examined with the corr() function whether continuous numeric variables have a bilateral relationship on the customer churn variable. Significant values close to 1.0 were not found. A few values are shown in Table 3.

With the Interactive Histogram module in Knime, scatter charts of the variables in terms of customer loss were drawn in Figure 2. Customers shown in green have not left the bank (variable Exited = 0). Customers shown in red are customers who have left the bank (variable Exited = 1).

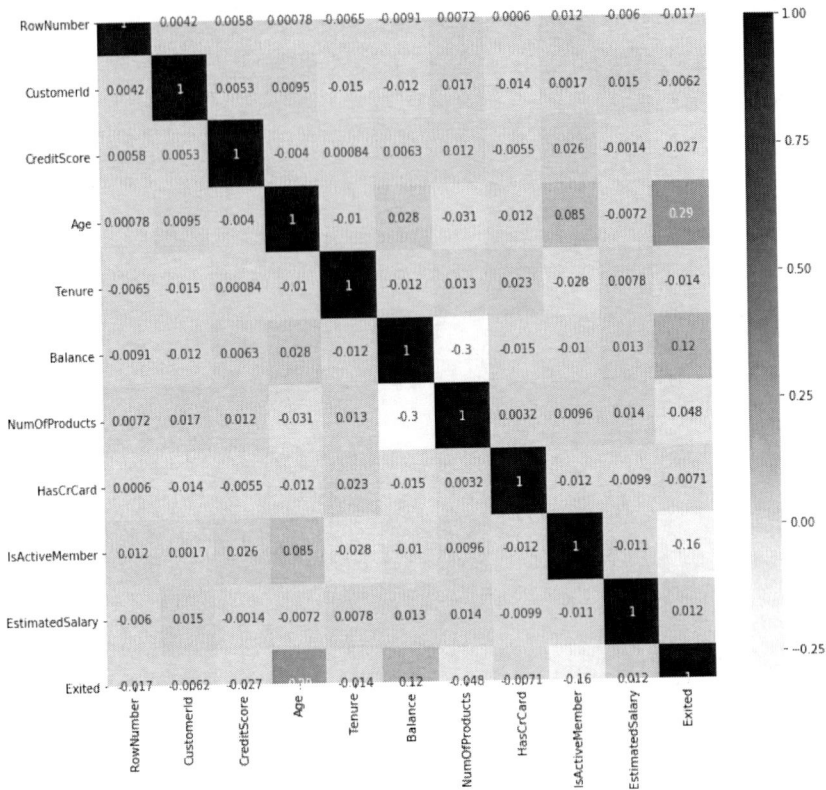

Figure 1. Correlation plot of variables.

Table 3. Variable correlation coefficients

Variables	Correlation coefficient
Customer's account balance amount (Balance)	0.11853276877163386
Usage time (Tenure)	-0.014000612253444594
Credit score (CreditScore)	-0.02709353975465778

The distribution of the age variable in terms of customer loss is shown with the histogram graph in Figure 3. We see that the number of customer losses in the 42-50 age range is higher than other age ranges. Then comes the 34-42 age range, the 50-58 age range and the 26-34 age range. In the 50-58 age range, we see a higher rate of separation compared to other ranges.

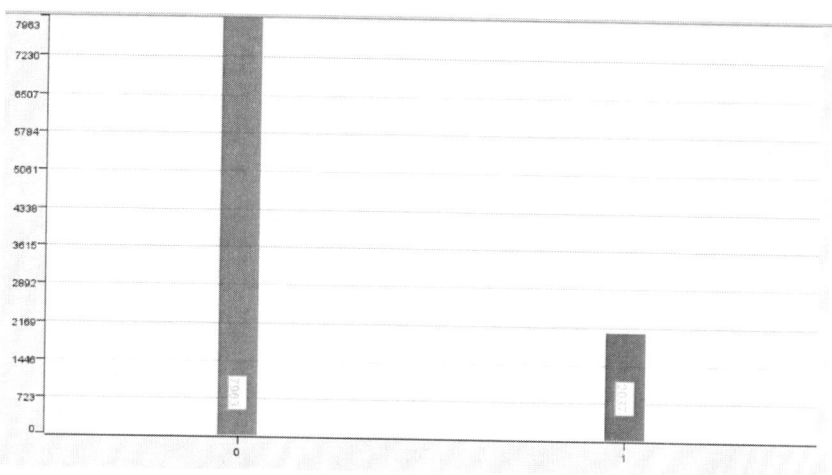

Figure 2. Loss of customers (0 = customer did not abandon, 1 = customer abandoned).

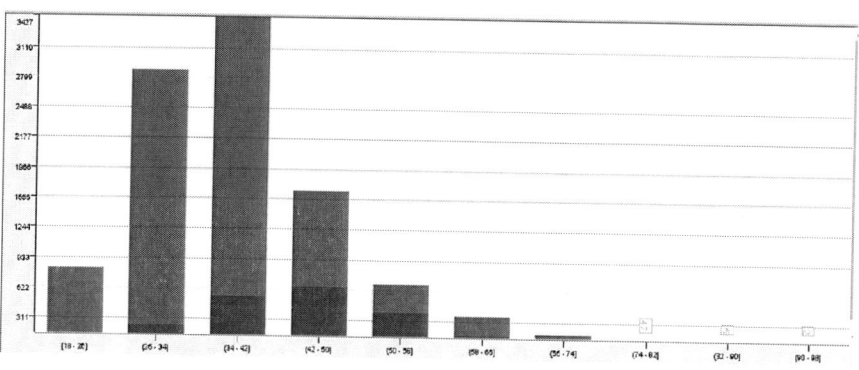

Figure 3. Customer loss distribution by age variable.

It is seen that the loss of customers is approximately evenly distributed in the number of years the bank has been a customer in Figure 4. When we look at the ratio, we see that the loss rate is lower for new customers between 0-2 years.

In Figure 5, it is shown that the number of customers with a balance of 0-41900,001 is higher and the loss rate is low compared to other ranges.

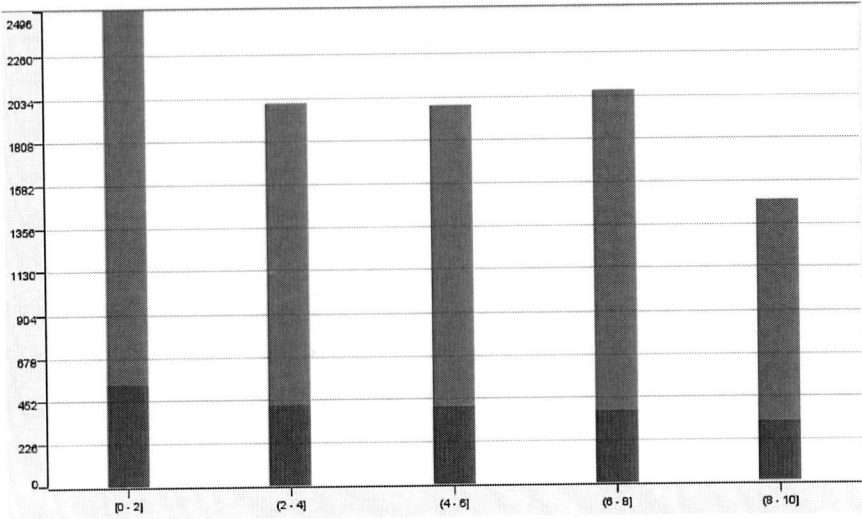

Figure 4. Distribution of number of years the customer has been a customer of the bank by loss of customers.

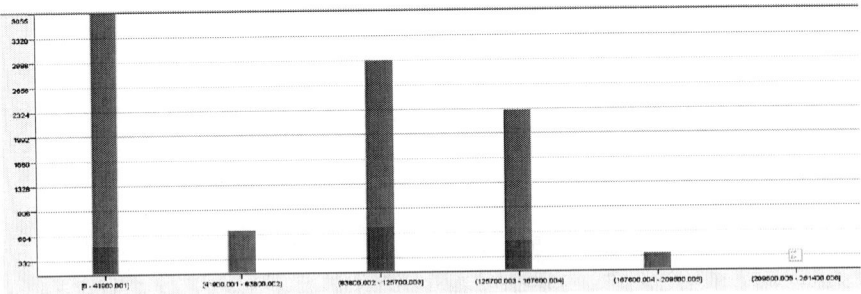

Figure 5. Customer loss distribution of customer's account balance amount.

Figure 6 shows that the rate of leaving the bank by active customers (1) is lower. In addition, it is seen that the number of active customers is higher.

It is seen that the loss of customers is approximately equal in every salary range in Figure 7.

There are 60 people with a used bank product of 4 and they are all abandoned customers. Figure 8 shows that customer loss is the highest proportionally, after 3, customers using 1 and 2 bank products.

Analysis of Customer Churn in the Banking Industry Using Data Mining

Figure 6. Distribution of customer loss by customer activity.

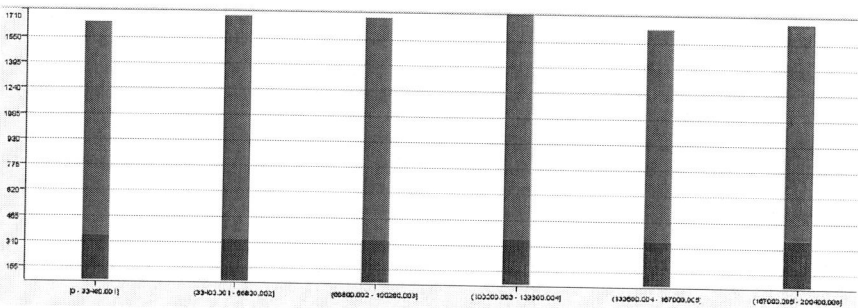

Figure 7. Customer loss distribution of estimated salary.

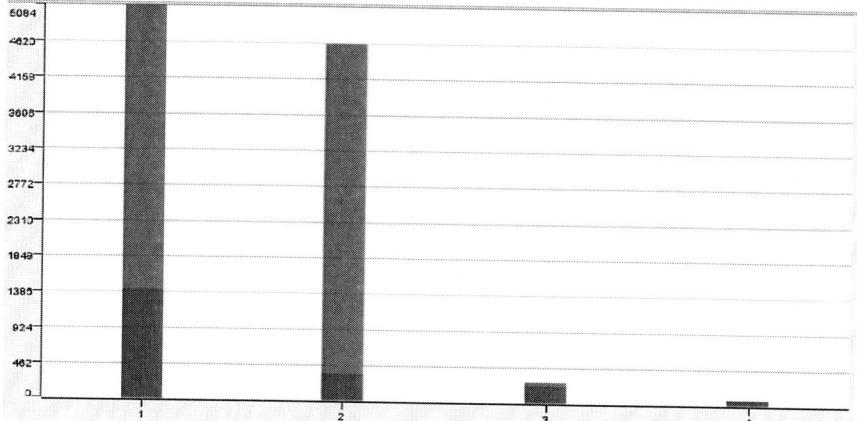

Figure 8. Distribution of number of bank products used by the customer by loss of customers.

Data Preparation

The next stage of data analysis is data cleaning, making it usable for the model. At this stage, the missing data in the data set is completed according to the determined rules. Unnecessary, unwanted customer number, surname, etc. variables are discarded. In this study, Knime was used, and the two variables mentioned with the Column Filter node were cleaned from the dataset.

The Exited variable, which is our target (Class) variable, has been converted into a string, that is, a categorical variable (string) with Number to String node so that we can use it in the analysis. With the same node, the variables of activity and credit card ownership were made categorical (string).

For a better analysis, new variables that are thought to be related to the data set can be derived and added to the data set. In this study, the T/NOP variable was produced, which indicates the ratio of the Usage time to the Number of Products Used variables (Tenure/NumOfProducts). A Math Formula node is used. Variables with continuous numerical values can be used in the model by dividing them into categories. Rule Engine node is used.

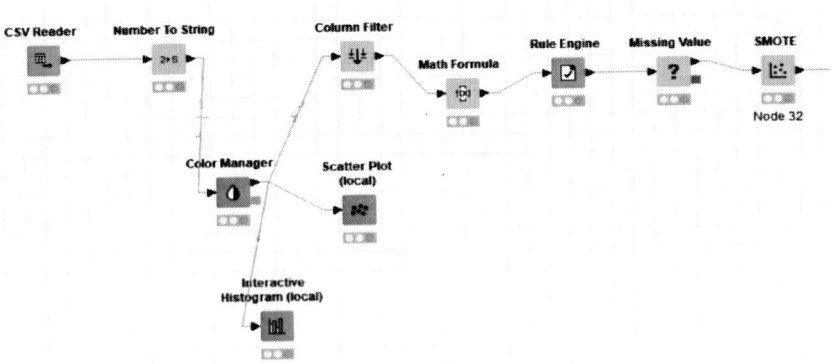

Figure 9. Data preparation and data understanding phase.

In the data set, it was seen that the number of customers who did not leave the bank was 7963, while the number of those who did was 2037. The big difference between these two numbers is something that can make the model difficult to learn. Therefore, the number of rows of the data set has been increased by generating and adding data with the same statistical information, without disturbing the structural features of the SMOTE node and the data set. SMOTE does not reproduce existing values. Creates new values based on the distance between existing values.

Data preprocessing steps can be further multiplied. The stages in this study are indicated. Figure 9 shows nodes in both data preparation and data understanding on Knime.

Data Modeling

After the Dataset Understanding and Preparation stages comes the Model creation stage. Various data mining algorithms that we will apply to the data we have prepared are selected, the parameters are determined, and the model is applied. When the model is ready, the accuracy value is calculated to measure the model success. The model emerges because of processing the data set with machine learning algorithms. Input information are hyperparameters that may differ for each algorithm that we have given to the model beforehand. The image shows its structure. In this study, Decision Tree, Random Forest, and Artificial Neural Networks algorithms were used.

Decision Tree Algorithm

Decision Tree algorithm is one of the supervised machine learning algorithms and is one of the most widely used classification algorithms. It is a predictive model, and its structure is easier and more understandable than other algorithms. The decision tree consists of nodes, the first node is the root node. Each node asks a question about itself and according to the answer given, it continues by connecting to another node as branches to the next nodes. When it comes to an end, leaves representing a class are reached. The decision tree consists of nested ifs.

The data set was divided into two as 70% for training and 30% for testing with Partition node. With the training part, the Decision Tree algorithm model was created. With the test data, the model estimated the target variable (class) and compared it with the actual values. Thus, model success metrics and Confusion Matrix were found. The matrix is shown in Table 4. The model was built on the Knime platform, and the model image is shown in Figure 10 along with the Random Forest algorithm model.

Table 4. The Confusion Matrix of the Decision Tree model

Estimated / real value	One	Zero
One	1044 (TP)	756 (FN)
Zero	579 (FP)	6621 (TN)

- True Positive (TP): True Positive => 1044
- False Negative (FN): False Negative => 756
- False Positive (FP): False Positive => 579
- True Negative (TN): True Negative => 6621

The Comparison Matrix given in Table 4, the model left the bank in the test data set, that is, the model correctly predicted 1044 data with a value of 1 for the Churn variable. Didn't leave the bank The model correctly predicted 6621 pieces of data with a value of 0 as the Churn variable. Model 1 predicted 756 with a true value of 1 and model 1 with a true value of 0 and 579 with a true value of 0. Based on this table, it is possible to easily measure the success of the model with various values.

- Model Accuracy *TP+TN/ Total:* This metric shows us the proportion of correct guesses among all predictions. The model gives its success. In this study, it was 0.852. It should be increased by working on the model.
- Precision of the Model (Precision) *TP/(TP+FP):* How many of those estimated to have abandoned did. It was found to be 0.64 in this study.
- Sharpness of Model (Recall) *TP/(TP+FN):* Indicates how many of the true abandoners were predicted. It is one of the most important metrics. 0.58 was found in this study. It is expected to be higher. It may be low due to the imbalance of 0 and 1 in the data set. It is necessary to increase the model by making improvements.
- Misclassification Rate *(FP+FN)/Total:* Error rate of the model. 14.83 was found.
- F1 score *2*Precision*Recall/(Precision*Recall):* It is a hybrid value of the two weighted averages of the Sensitivity and Sharpness metrics. It is beneficial to evaluate the two criteria together. 0.61 was found.

- Cohen's kappa coefficient of the model (Cohen's Kappa): It shows the consistency and agreement between the categorical answer options. 0.519 found in this study

The Random Forest Algorithm

Random Forest is one of the supervised machine learning algorithms and is a powerful tool for classification problems. The random forest algorithm allows us to generate multiple trees. It is based on decision trees. It reduces the problem of over-learning and overfitting, which is one of the biggest problems of random forest decision trees. Each tree consists of the nodes in the decision trees, the branches that connect them, and the leaves, which are the result. The random forest provides a wider variety of modeling possibilities than the decision tree algorithm. The main advantage of the random forest algorithm is that it is very useful and easy to use. The number of hyperparameters we have given is not much and is understandable.

It can give importance to variables. It indicates which variable is the root node most frequently and shows the importance of this variable. In the bank customer churn study, the variable that emerged the most root node was repeated 28 times and became the Number of Product Usage variable. This variable is the most important primary variable that is used most when making the first distinction in trees. The most recurrent variable was Age. The decision maker can use it to guide their decisions by disabling variables that are less repetitive or giving importance to those that are highly repetitive.

In the Random Forest Decision Tree study, the model with the best accuracy value was tried to be created by experimenting with hyperparameters. As a result of the trials, information gain was determined as the split criterion, the limit number of levels of the trees was determined as 10, and the minimum number of nodes (minimum node size) was determined as 4. The number of trees is the most important hyperparameter. While the high number of trees increases the efficiency, it slows down the time. Therefore, the number of models was determined as 100. The model was created with these values and Table 5 gives the Confusion Matrix.

As in the Decision Tree, the data set was divided into two for 70% training and 30% testing with Partition node. A Random Forest algorithm model was created with the training part. With the test data, the model estimated the target variable (class) and compared it with the actual values. Thus, model success metrics and Confusion Matrix were found. Table 3 shows the matrix.

Table 5. The complexity matrix of the Random Forest model (Confusion Matrix)

Estimated / real value		One	Zero
One		762 (TP)	1038(FN)
Zero		183 (FP)	7017(TN)

- True Positive (TP): True Positive => 762
- False Negative (FN): False Negative => 1038
- False Positive (FP): False Positive => 183
- True Negative (TN): True Negative => 7017

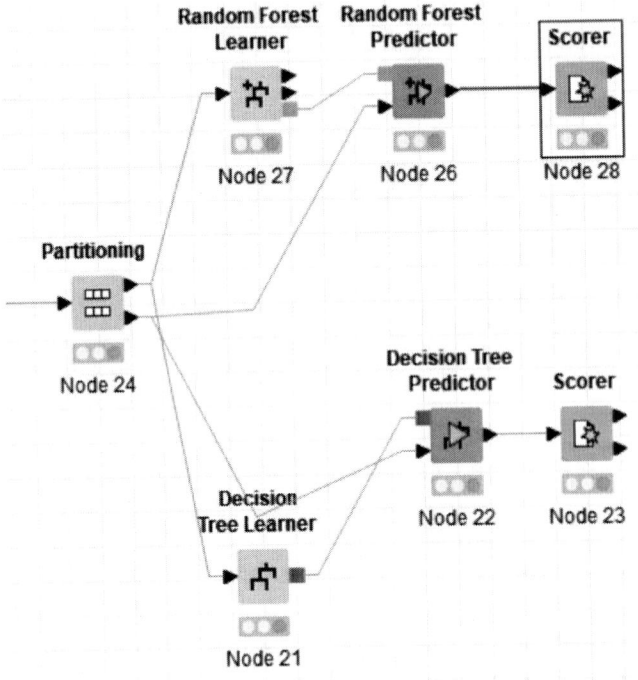

Figure 10. Decision Tree and Random Forest algorithm models.

The confusion matrix in Table 5 shows that the model left the bank in the test data set, that is, 762 data with a value of 1 for the Churn variable were correctly predicted as model 1. In terms of not to leave the ban, the model correctly predicted 7017 pieces of data with a value of 0 for the Churn variable. An incorrect estimation has been made by estimating 1038 with a true value of 1 and model 0 with a true value of 183 with the model 1.

- The Accuracy value of the model was found to be 0.864.
- The Precision value of the model was found to be 0.806.
- The Sharpness (Recall) value of the model was found to be 0.423.
- The Misclassification Rate of the model was found to be 13,567.
- F1 score: 0.555 was found.
- Cohen's kappa coefficient of the model (Cohen's Kappa): 0.484 was found.

The model set up on the Knime platform is shown in Figure 10.

Artificial Neural Networks

Artificial Neural Networks is an algorithm inspired by neurons and synapses, which are the working logic of the human brain. In this algorithm, connections are formed between artificial nerve cells and cells. There is an input layer, an output layer, and there are hidden layers between them. The parameters of how many layers and neurons should be determined in advance. There is no definite rule, the appropriate number is given by trial and error. In hidden layers there are neurons in the layer. Input layer has input(x) and output layer has target (class) variables which we call output(y). The relationship between them is y=f(x)+Error. To reduce the error weight (weight)(W) information is found and assigned. The purpose here is to perform the operation with the inputs by performing an operation according to the importance of the inputs. This is the activation function.

These elements are present in the structure of artificial neural networks, inputs, weights, summation function, activation function and outputs. The working logic is the formation of the learning algorithm by finding the binding weights (w) of the input elements. Explaining the results of this algorithm is more difficult than explaining the result of a linear model. Algorithm layer image is given in Figure 11. (Çınar, 2018)

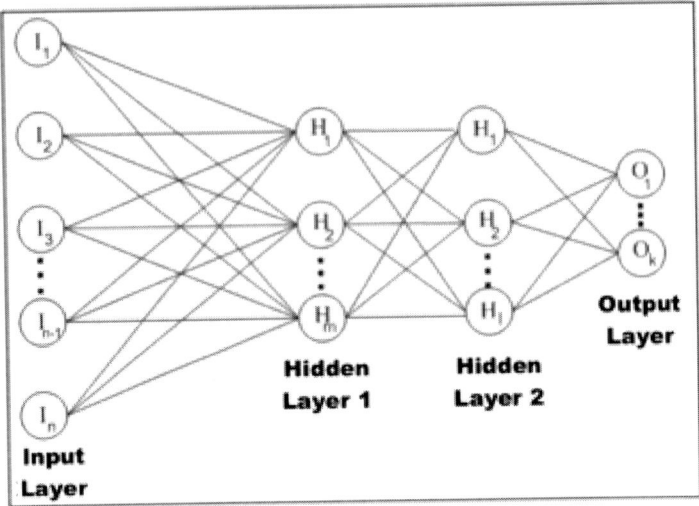

Figure 11. Artificial Neural Network example.

In artificial neural networks, data is used by normalizing. All data types must be numeric for the data to be normalized. Categorical (string) converted all input (input data) variables to numeric type with Category to Number node. The target (class) variable is left categorical (string). The data were normalized using the normalizer node and the z-score. Artificial neural network algorithm cannot be established without normalizing the data. With the partitioning node, the data was divided into two for 70% training and 30% for testing. The model was built with the training part, then the model was tested with the test data. The Artificial Neural Network model made in Knime is given in Figure 12. Table 4 gives the Confusion Matrix.

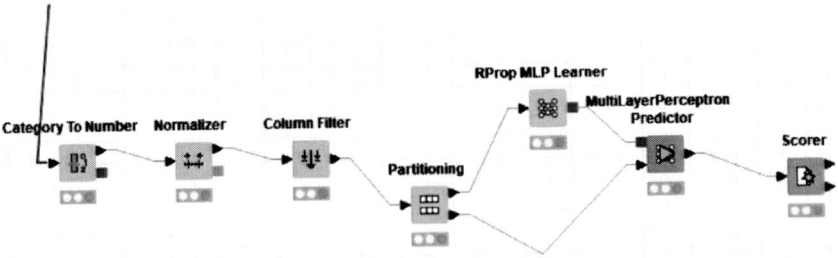

Figure 12. Artificial Neural Network algorithm model.

Table 6. Complexity matrix of Artificial Neural Network model (Confusion Matrix)

Estimated \ real value	One	Zero
One	889 (TP)	944 (FN)
Zero	303 (FP)	6864 (TN)

- True Positive (TP): True Positive => 889
- False Negative (FN): False Negative => 944
- False Positive (FP): False Positive => 303
- True Negative (TN): True Negative => 6864

When we look at the Confusion Matrix given in Table 6, the model left the bank in the test data set, that is, the model correctly predicted 889 data with a value of 1 for the Churn variable. The model did not leave the bank. The model correctly predicted 6864 data with a value of 0. Model 0 with a true value of 1, 944 with a true value of 0, and 303 with a true value of 0, predicted model 1.

- The Accuracy value of the model was found to be 0.861.
- The Precision value of the model was found to be 0.746.
- The Sharpness (Recall) value of the model was found to be 0.485.
- The Misclassification Rate of the model was found to be 13,856.
- F1 score: 0.588 was found.

Cohen's kappa coefficient (Cohen's Kappa) of the model was found to be 0.509.

Conclusion

In the study, data mining models were created that predict which bank customers will leave the bank and which will not. The data comprehension phase was done with Python programming language, and then the model was created on the Knime platform. The data set used was divided into two. While the model was created with the training part, the accuracy values of the model were found with the test part. Algorithms used in modeling; Decision Tree

(Random Forest) and Artificial Neural Networks (Artificial Neural Networks). The truth value comparison table of these algorithms is given in table 7.

Table 7. Comparing algorithm metrics

	Accuracy	Sharpness (Recall)
Decision Tree	0.852	0.581
Random Forest	0.864	0.423
Artificial Neural Networks (Artificial Neural Networks)	0.861	0.485

According to table 7, the Accuracy value is a random forest algorithm, albeit with slight differences. Another important metric is the decision tree algorithm with the highest Recall value. The values found do not indicate that the success of the model is at a sufficient level. Model success rates can be increased by making changes on the hyperparameters used in the models, adding new variables to the data set, cleaning the extra variables, or making other changes on the model.

Making bank churn analyses of the bank's customers enables us to see the customers who are likely to leave the existing customers. This is very important information in terms of Customer Relationship Management and Marketing activities of the relevant bank. You should not think only for banking. Customer loss analysis is valuable for telecommunications, mobile as well as other gaming channels, mobile applications, e-commerce sites and many other companies. While the customer churn action is certain for companies with subscription logic such as banking and telecommunications, the situation may be different for other sectors. For example, an e-commerce site "in the last x months must create the data set by specifying certain conditions such as "customers who have not made any transactions." The same may be true for banks. Determining the customer churn value according to the average time between transactions can be attributed to different conditions than net situations such as account closure and card cancellation.

The effort and cost to acquire a new customer are greater than the cost of retaining an existing customer. For this reason, companies need to carry out activities to prevent loss of customers and loyalty programs. Firms will focus on a more limited customer group, knowing in advance the customers who are likely to leave. This will provide both ease of operation and cost advantage.

The activities that the companies can do by making use of the estimation results of the customer churn probability obtained in this study are listed below.

- Customer churn rates can be reduced by making various campaigns for customers who are likely to leave the company. Customers' reactions to studies on such customers can also be recorded in the database, and new data sets can be created and new analyzes can be created. Thus, the success rates of the activity emerge. It can be a guide for future campaigns.
- Reminding the most prominent features or services of the company to customers who are likely to leave the company can be done via SMS, pop-up, notification, or any other method. Recommendation Engines, which are data analysis algorithms, can be used to determine which feature will be recommended or reminded to which customer. As stated in the previous article, the customer's reactions should be recorded in the database so that they can be analyzed in future studies.
- Companies should regularly analyze customer loss and the results should be shared with the departments. With the automatic mailing node in Knime used in this study, the authorities can see the people who are likely to leave the company, for example, once every 4 months during the year.
- Intra-company strategies can be created by paying attention to the priority variables found in the Random Forest algorithm.
- By taking the abandoned customers into a separate data set, their common features can be analyzed. With different data analysis algorithms, the reasons for customer loss can be revealed by comparing the customers who do not leave and who do not.

References

Alaybeg, F., 2019. Data Mining Introduction, Methods and Methodologies. *Medium.* https://furkanalaybeg.medium.com/veri-madencili%C4%9Fi-ve-y%C3%B6ntemleri-d0e2fd238e44.

Çınar, U., 2018. *Neural Networks and Application with R Program.* https://www.veribilimiokulu.com/yapay-sinir-aglari/.

Doğan, B., Erol B. and Buldu, A., 2014. Using the Association Rule for Customer Relationship Management in the Insurance Industry. *International Journal of Advances in Engineering and Pure Sciences* 3, 105-114.

Gulpinar, V., 2013. Customer Loss Analysis in Turkish Telecommunications Market with the Help of Artificial Neural Networks and Social Network Analysis. *Marmara University Journal of Economics and Administrative Sciences* 34 (1), 331-350.

Gupta, D. and Kamilla, U., 2014. Cyber Banking in India: A Cross-Sectional Analysis Using Structural Equation Model. *IUP Journal of Bank Management* 13 (2).

Gürsoy, U. Ş., 2010. Customer Churn Analysis in Telecommunication Sector. *Journal of Istanbul University Faculty of Business* 39 (1), 35–49.

Hsieh, N. C., 2004. An Integrated Data Mining and Behavioral Scoring Model for Analyzing Bank Customers. *Expert Systems with Applications* 27 (4), 623–633.

Ivanchenko, O., Mirgorodskaya, O. N., Baraulya, E. V. and Putilina T. I., 2019. Marketing Relations and Communication Infrastructure Development in the Banking Sector Based on Big Data Mining. *International Journal of Economics and Business Administration* 7, 176-184.

Maryani, I. and Riana, D., 2017. Clustering and Profiling of Customers Using RFM for Customer Relationship Management Recommendations. In 2017 5th *International Conference on Cyber and IT Service Management* (CITSM), 1-6.

Mukherjee, A. and Nath, P., 2003. A Model of Trust in Online Relationship Banking. *International Journal of Bank Marketing* 5, 5-15.

Parviainen, P., Tihinen M., Kääriäinen J. and Teppola, S. 2017. Tackling the Digitalization Challenge: How to Benefit from Digitalization in Practice. *International Journal of Information Systems and Project Management* 5 (1), 63-77.

Payne, A., 2005. *Handbook of CRM*. Routledge.

Sassen, S., 2000. *Globalization and Its Discontents: Essays on the New Mobility of People and Money*. New York: NewPress.

Savaşçı, I. and Tatlıdil R., 2006. The Effect of the Crm (Customer Relationship Management) Strategy Applied by the Banks in the Credit Card Market on Customer Loyalty. *Aegean Journal of Academic Perspective* 6 (1), 62-73.

Şimşek, H., 2018. Machine Learning Lessons 5a: Random Forest (Classification). *Veri Bilimi Türkiye. [Data Science Turkey]*.https://medium.com/data-science-en/machine-%C3%B6%C4%9Frenmesi-desleri-5-bagging-ve-random-forest-2f803cf21e07.

Vafeiadis, T., Diamantaras, K. I., Sarigiannidis, G. and Chatzisavvas K. C., 2015. A Comparison of Machine Learning Techniques for Customer Churn Prediction. *Simulation Modeling Practice and Theory* 55, 1-9.

Wijaya, A. and Girsang, A. S., 2015. Use of Data Mining for Prediction of Customer Loyalty. *CommIT (Communication and Information Technology) Journal* 10 (1), 41-47.

Chapter 5

The Crowdsourcing Concept-Based Data Mining Approach Applied in Prosumer Microgrids

B. C. Neagu*, PhD, M. Gavrilaș, PhD, O. Ivanov, PhD and G. Grigoraș
Department of Power Engineering, "Gheorghe Asachi" Technical University, Iasi, Romania

Abstract

Energy efficiency is a tool for saving money and resources, representing a necessity for flexible adaptation to users' demands. Because the use of electricity plays a fundamental role in modern lifestyles, users' load characteristics must reflect the people's lives at work and leisure. The future microgrids must ensure "smart" features like flexibility, accessibility, reliability, and high power quality for all consumers. Increased adoption of small-scale distributed energy sources (SSDES) helps lead to the decarbonisation of microgrids. Presently, with more prominent reason, society requires to ensure that the benefits of smart electricity are conceivable to the total and that the benefit is given in a clean and effective manner. Energy poverty is described as a lack of access to clean and affordable energy, resulting in soaring energy costs. The crowdsourcing concept, introduced by J. Surowiecki in 2005, is used to mitigate energy scarcity. It can be a useful tool for allowing the crowd to do community service within a specific geographic region. According to Romania's Energy Regulation National Agency's Order No. 228 launched on December 28, 2018, the prosumers can sell the energy

---

* Corresponding Author's Email: bogdan.neagu@tuiasi.ro.

In: The Future of Data Mining
Editor: Cem Ufuk Baytar
ISBN: 979-8-88697-250-4
© 2022 Nova Science Publishers, Inc.

produced SSDES on the free market. Many advanced trading models have as the goal increasing the benefits of the peers that sell energy in local community market. Many researchers considered this field challenging and significant to be investigated. Knowledge Discovery in Databases (KDD) or Data Mining (DM) is the effort to understand, analyse, and use a high amount of the available data. The main aim of this paper is to quantify the distortion effects and introduce a stringent and comprehensive methodology integrating the distribution network operator (DNO), prosumers, and consumers. Based on aforementioned considerations, an efficient and robust data mining-based methodology is proposed to identify the power system cost saved by the residential consumers when prosumers act to maximize their profit, and the DNOs act to maximize the benefit resulted from an optimal operation of the electricity distribution networks.

Keywords: crowdsourcing, data mining, prosumer, microgrids

Introduction

Increasing energy demand and the threat of global warming lead to the exploitation of additional and cleaner energy sources. A consequence of this trend is the growing penetration of SSDES. These installations may now belong to microgrid consumers, which become prosumers, i.e., both producers and consumers of energy. Photovoltaic (PV) panels, in particular, had significant growth in recent years, with incentives given by EU countries like Romania (see Law no. 184/2018), motivating its adoption and turning it into a business case. The support of bidirectional power flows resulting from the transactive energy in the local communities, as well as the need to decrease the power loss lead to changes of the microgrids, namely in Low Voltage (LV) distribution, pointing in the direction of a more responsive and efficient Smart Grids (SGs).

Energy efficiency is a tool for saving money and resources, representing a necessity for flexible adaptation to users' demands. Because the use of electricity plays a fundamental role in modern lifestyles; users' load characteristics must reflect the people's lives at work and leisure. The volume of available information and necessary for the operation, management, planning, and security of the microgrids have gradually increased with technological development, requiring the introduction of the calculation technique and intelligent solutions, Piccinini et al., (2015). Even if the prosumers have high benefits, their behavior is intermittent, and, for this reason, the DNOs must consider a comprehensive microgrid planning strategy. Moreover, they should be able to function both connected and independently (autonomously) to the grid Andoni et al., (2010). Developed for communities, the microgrids integrate local electricity production to satisfy the exact demand of the consumers. The active consumers and prosumers are defined in the context of recent paradigms of energy independence, energy policy, and distributive management.

The microgrids is seen as the instrument to perform a coordinate structure for fair integration of SSDES, which will be an edifying challenge for DNOs that will require another operation plan. The prosumers form the active cells of the microgrids in which any cell can supply installations to the DNO to optimize the capacity of grid hosting and hence SSRES implementation in a profitable and efficient operating way Espe et al., (2018).

In Romania, energy efficiency is improved from the increasing electricity amounts generated by small producers (prosumers) with installed power up to 27 kW. These amounts are traded directly to the provider with which a bilateral contract has already been signed Neagu et al., (2020a).

The prosumer's behavior must be a balanced one to store power surplus when low demand spells and deliver it during the demand increases Diahovchenko et al., (2020). An up-to-date report published by the European Union - Smart Grids Task Force, Final report (2020), adds an explicit direction to build a smart meter (SM) roadmap to satisfy the necessities of the future energy markets through a modular and resilient structure for the metering architecture. Thus, the SM should ensure helpful information on the shape of the prosumers' load Chicco et al., (2020).

The proliferation of SSDES changes both the operating conditions and management requirements of the microgrids, which must now integrate new technologies and procedures. In recent years, the SG concept has been implemented in several scales and initiatives in Romania, with much of the hardware already tested and approved, albeit in isolation. In this context, an assumption of a framework or unifying architecture of interfaces and protocols based on norms and standards is essential. Thus, a reference architecture for the data exchange between devices and electrical systems must be defined, allowing the products, services, protocols, and interfaces to interact Kazmi et al., (2017); Deng et al., (2017). Figure 1 illustrates the transition from classical electricity grids to microgrids.

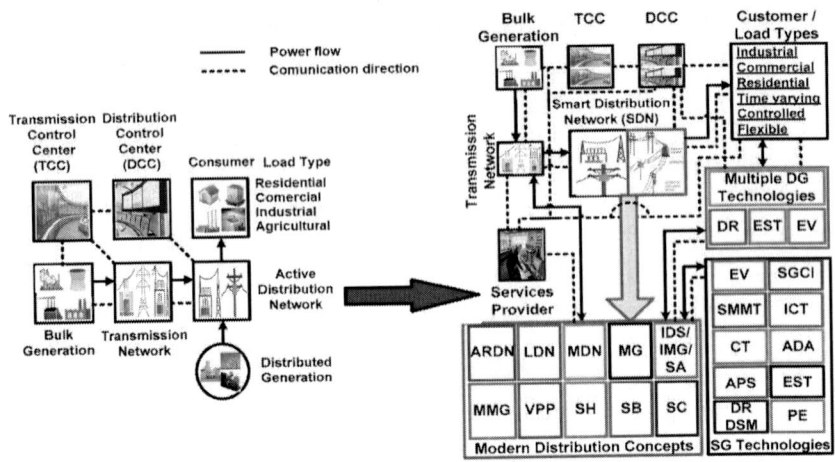

Figure 1. The transition from classical grids to microgrids.

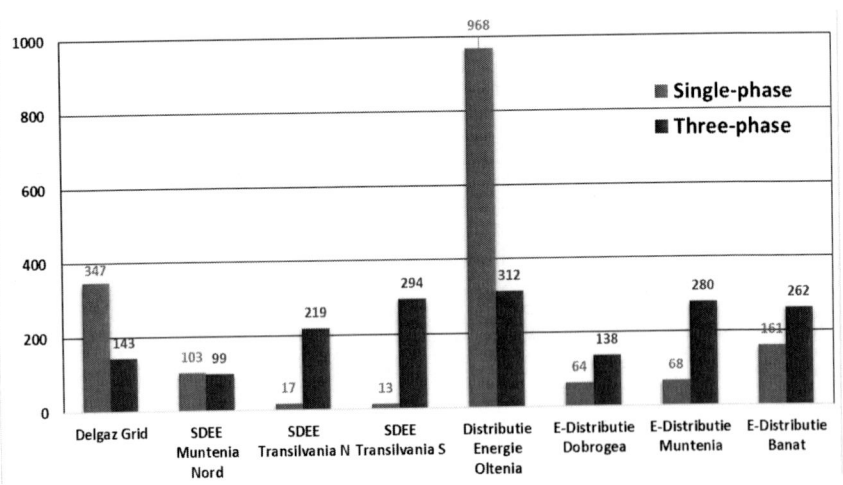

Figure 2. The number of prosumers from each DSOs of Romania.

The increasing number of prosumers with various distributed energy recourses promotes the peer-to-peer (P2P) energy transaction in the smart grid for less cost, more flexibility, lower carbon footprints, and higher reliability. Recent research on the prosumers' behavior in the electric distribution systems has increased in recent years. A distributed privacy-preserving P2P energy transaction approach has been proposed to minimize the overall objective of renewable generation curtailment penalty, adjustment cost, and operation cost while satisfying linearized distribution network power flow, power line thermal, and voltage limit constraints. In the last two years, the prosumers' integration in the microgrids has become an actual problem in Romania, with the national government encouraging this process through incentives. For example, Figure 2 shows the number of the over 3500 prosumers connected in low voltage distribution networks for all Romanian DNOs Neagu et al., (2020b). In this context, the prosumers' behavior becomes a pressing issue for aggregators, providers, and DNOs.

The system for promoting the production of renewable energy is established by Law 184/2018. It represents an important step in the regulation of prosumers' status in Romania. This legislative framework provides for a series of advantages, as follows (in accordance with the 228/2018 Order of the Romanian National Regulatory Authority for Energy):

- the scheme is applied to prosumers owning renewable energy production units with an installed capacity of not more than 27 kW per consumption place in individual households, residential blocks, residential, commercial or industrial areas;
- the electricity distribution operators must connect prosumers following the specific regulations issued by the regulatory authority in this respect;
- prosumers have the possibility of selling electricity to suppliers with whom they have concluded electricity supply contracts at a price equaling the weighted average price recorded on the day-ahead market in the previous year; suppliers having an agreement with prosumers must take over the energy at the former's request;
- exemption of prosumers from the payment of excise duties for the amount of electricity produced from renewable sources for self-consumption, and the excess production sold to suppliers;
- exemption of prosumers as natural persons from the obligation of purchasing green certificates annually and quarterly for the electricity produced and used for own final consumption, other than own technological consumption of power plants;
- benefiting from the regularisation service between the value of electricity delivered and the value of electricity consumed in the grid by the electricity suppliers with whom they have concluded electricity supply contracts the service.

According to the above regulations, the electricity suppliers bound by contracts with prosumers request to buy the electricity at the weighted average day-ahead market price from the previous year. Thus, the prosumer can sell on the market its electricity surplus, while the advantage for the supplier is the exemption from the payment of the distribution network tariff. The trading system offers a basic solution, having limitations regarding the options for both parts (prosumers want to sell and consumers to buy electricity at lower prices). It does not account for differences in generation costs and installed capacity by not allowing prosumers to set custom selling prices. The incentive of increasing local generation is not present. Consumers cannot buy electricity directly from the prosumers, thus not having the freedom to choose specific prosumers for trading Neagu et al., (2020c).

Many advanced trading models have as the goal increasing the benefits of the peers that trade electricity in the local market of microgrids (LMM). A comprehensive methodology for optimal integration of prosumers to minimize active power losses in microgrids is proposed in the chapter. For a deeper analysis regarding the influence of the prosumers on the microgrid power losses, the 24-hour real load consumption and generation profiles are obtained using a data mining process.

Crowdsourcing Energy System

The mitigation of energy poverty Neagu et al., (2020d) can be achieved using crowdsourcing, a concept first introduced in 2005 by Surowiecki et al., (2005). Crowdsourcing, Maxim et al., (2016), represents an emerging trend that integrates contributions from users and the collective wisdom of the crowd, Howe et al., (2006). It is very important to build a service-based approach to make these crowdsourced sensor cloud data available. It can also be an effective means to enable the crowd to provide a service-sharing community within a geographical area by using their smartphones, Alt et al., (2010). Users can take advantage of services from their neighborhood users through this crowdsourced service community. Since the crowd (i.e., service providers) is mobile, the availability of crowdsourced services to users is limited to its spatio-temporal adjacency, i.e., both service providers and users should be within a spatial region at a particular time.

A key issue is selecting and composing services from such a large number of everchanging crowdsourced sensor cloud services to fulfill users' requirements in a real-time fashion and based on spatio-temporal features. As a result, new spatio-temporal service selection and composition technologies are key approaches to leverage spatio-temporal crowdsourcing as a service provisioning platform.

A crowdsourced energy system (see Figure 3) includes a plurality of distributed energy resources managed by crowdsources of the system, a power network to which the distributed energy resources are connected, and a system operator that manages energy trading transactions and energy delivery within the system, the system operator operating at least one computing device configured to obtain day-ahead peer-to-peer energy trading transaction requests from crowdsources for energy to be delivered from the distributed energy resources, estimate day-ahead energy load and solar forecasts, determine optimal power flow for the delivery of energy, and schedule delivery of energy from the distributed energy resources across the power network based upon the energy trading transaction requests, the estimated forecasts, and the determined optimal power flow.

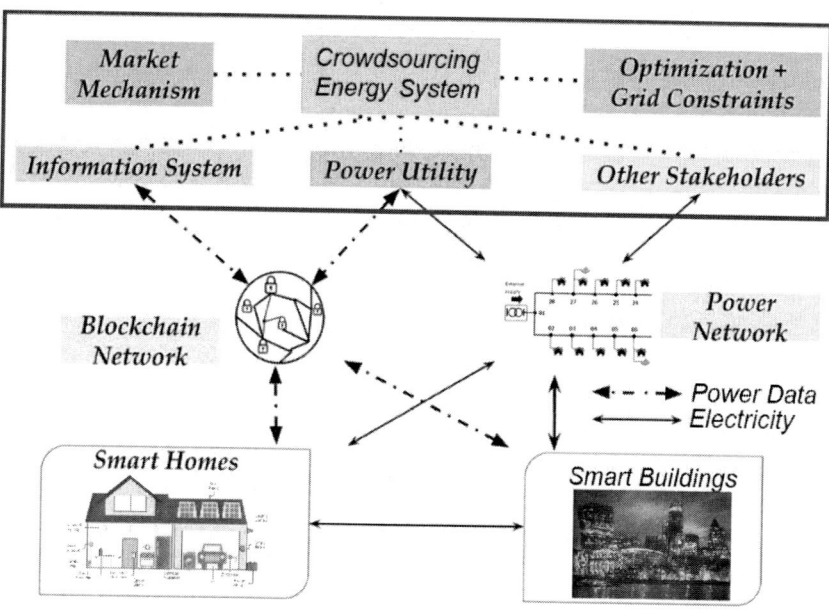

Figure 3. A particular model for crowdsourcing energy system.

It can be an effective means to enable the crowd to provide community service within a geographical area. In recent years, billions of dollars have been invested in the research on blockchain technology to make the most of its potential and understand how appropriate it is in the different economic domains Mika et al., (2020). Nevertheless, not all fields are fully ready to assimilate blockchain technology. The current technological opportunities must be analyzed in each particular case together with the challenges that the end-users face and with how a new decentralized architecture could create value for them Wang et al., (2019).

Fortunately, the electricity industry is a suitable candidate for innovation through blockchain technology. It integrates a complex supply chain with needs to increase transparency and improved data management. In addition, it contains a highly transactional trading market that would benefit from instant settlement Unguru, (2018). The clarity and immutability of the blockchain can empower end-users of this industry and consumers.

The Problem Formulation

The Prosumer Profiling Using Data Mining Method

The innovations in information technology have made it possible to acquire and store large data amounts. Many activity fields, including the electricity, are becoming increasingly dependent on data collection, storage, and processing. However, the excess of data encounters difficulties in finding the features that correspond to a specific objective. Due to the rapid increase of the number and size of databases, it is necessary to examine and to propose techniques for the automatic extraction of knowledge from these large size databases. Many researchers considered this field challenging and significant to be investigated. Knowledge Discovery in Databases (KDD) or Data Mining (DM) is the effort to understand, analyse, and use a high amount of the available data. Thus, a new research direction emerged that supported the analysis of information extracted from existing data in databases, called data mining. Generally, Data Mining represents a data analysis process to extract useful information used to optimize performance indicators. There are situations when a DNO has a large-size database, and a human operator could not process it efficiently. Through applying a Data Mining algorithm, the "hidden" features are discovered easily. These techniques can understand patterns and apply them in feature selection using proper algorithms. The features extracted from the databases are used in predictive models, understanding the relationships between records or contents associated with the database Neagu et al., (2020b).

The research on the prosumers' behaviour in the microgrids has increased in the last years mainly due to the uncertain nature of the active power injection into the network. If the difference between the generation and the consumption of the prosumers is unknown, it can cause undesirable effects on the optimal operation and planning of the microgrids. An efficient and robust methodology based on the mining data techniques was proposed in the paper to identify the behavioural characteristics of the prosumers from the microgrids. There are three categories where the Data mining techniques can be grouped, depending on the type of problem:

- Classification and regression. It represents the most common category of applications, consisting of building the forecasting models belonging to a set of classes (classification) or regression values). From this category, the following approaches can be applied with success: decision trees, the Bayes technique, neural networks, and K-Nearest Neighbours.
- The analysis of associations and successions. This category generates descriptive models that highlight correlation rules between the attributes of a data set.
- Cluster analysis. It obtains the groups with similar entities or highlights the entities that differ substantially from a group.

Figure 4 presents the main steps of Data Mining-based analysis. The following operations take place inside each step Neagu et al., (2020b):

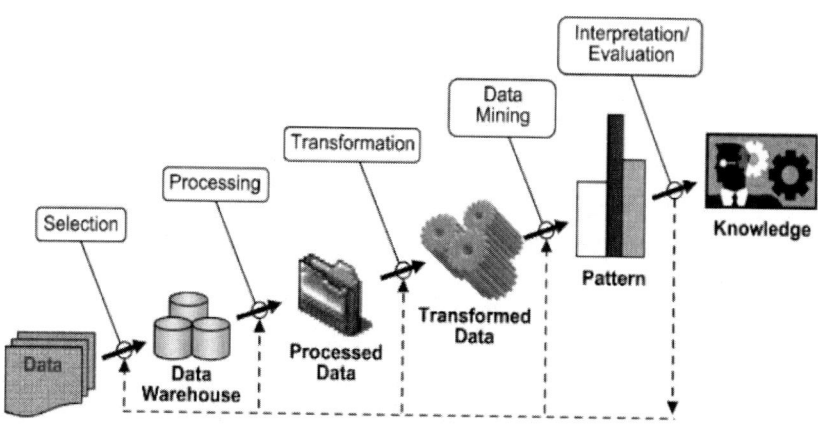

Figure 4. The components of the distribution service quality.

Data cleaning supposes a removal of irrelevant or "atypical" data;

Data integration considers the data sources integrated into the Data Mining process. A common trend in information applications is to perform data cleaning and integration as a pre-processing step, in which the storage of resulting data is done in a data warehouse;

Data selection. The significant features are identified to be used in the next step;

Data Normalization. Data are transformed or consolidated into forms suitable for the data mining process;

Data Mining. It represents the essential process in which intelligent methods are applied to extract patterns from data. K-means clustering method was chosen in the power quality analysis being most used in the scientific and industrial applications;

Pattern Evaluation. This step is necessary to identify the knowledge based on particular measures of their degree of interest;

Knowledge presentation. Visualization and presentation techniques are used to present to the Decision-Maker the discovered knowledge.

Optimal Allocation of Prosumers in Local Microgrids

The solution for the optimal location of small-scale renewable energy sources (SSRES) uses a simulation algorithm based on iterative computation of steady state, in order to minimize losses from the microgrid. The main objective is the optimal location of generation sources minimize energy losses in a microgrid. In essence, for a radial distribution network with N nodes, knowing its structure, the optimization variables refer to the capacity of the distributed generators known a priori, located in the nodes of the microgrid. In a first phase, all the generation sources are located in each node of the microgrid. The optimization variables are included in the column vector x whose length is equal to the number of nodes, $x = [x_1, x_2, ..., x_N]^t$ where t is used for transpose the vector. The inputs x_i, $(I = 1,...,N)$, represent a discrete value of the of capacity size of the SSRES connected in a random node i (zero if the SSRES is not present).

The optimization model considers the variation of the SSRES generated power and the active and reactive load consumed. The considered analysis timescale is divided into H time intervals Δt_h, for any $h = 1,...,H$. Neagu et al., (2019).

The objective function is to minimize the energy losses indicated by $\Delta P_h^{(d)}$ - the active power losses on each branch $d = 1, ..., D$ in the time interval $h = 1, ..., H$:

$$\min = F(\mathbf{x}) = \sum_{h=1}^{H}\sum_{d=1}^{D} \Delta P_h^{(d)}(\mathbf{x}) \cdot \Delta t_h \qquad (1)$$

However, a high degree of prosumers penetration can have a considerable impact on power flows, increasing the voltage and power losses. Equality restrictions are given by the equations of power flows; for any node $i = 1, ..., N$ and for each time interval ($h = 1, ..., H$), the equation is:

$$P_h^{(i)} + jQ_h^{(i)} = \bar{U}_h^{(i)} \bar{I}_h^{(i)*} \qquad (2)$$

The inequality restrictions complete the optimization method with the following:

1. Voltage variation limits:

$$U_{h,\min}^{(i)} \leq U_{i,h} \leq U_{h,\max}^{(i)} \qquad (3)$$

where $U_{h,\min}^{(i)}$ and $U_{h,\max}^{(i)}$ are the minimum and maximum effective value of the voltage for bus $I = 1, ..., N$ at $h = 1, ..., H$.

2. Branch thermal limits: the effective value of the current over the brach $d = 1, ..., D$, at hour $h = 1, ..., H$, denoted as $I_h^{(d)}$, must be less than the maximum admissible current for the line, $I_{h,\min}^{(d)}$:

$$I_h^{(d)} \leq I_{h,\max}^{(d)} \qquad (4)$$

3. Generation limits: power generated by SSRES at bus $I = 1, ..., N$ in hour $h = 1, ..., H$, $P_h^{(i,SSRES)}$, is less than the maximum power allowed at bus, $P_{h,\max}^{(i,SSRES)}$:

$$P_h^{(i,SSRES)} \leq P_{h,\max}^{(i,SSRES)} \tag{5}$$

4. Constraints for reactive power in SSRES bus:

$$Q_{h,\min}^{(i,SSRES)} \leq Q_h^{(i,SSRES)} \leq Q_{h,\max}^{(i,SSRES)} \tag{6}$$

where $Q_{h,\min}^{(i,SSRES)}$ and $Q_{h,\max}^{(i,SSRES)}$ are minimum/maximum allowable reactive power of SSRES, and $Q_h^{(i,SSRES)}$ is the reactive power of SSRES in bus $I = 1,\ldots,N$ at hour $h = 1,\ldots,H$.

The simulation search is used in the methodology by trying all permutations of SSRES placements for the microgrid busses. The objective function (1) is utilized in this example. Each alternative must be validated in order to verify if the solution agrees to the restrictions. Validation of solutions is required for each combination of SSRES locations through the following steps: (i) power flow computation and elimination of solutions that result in at least one restriction violation at one or more hours, (ii) objective function evaluation for feasible solutions that do not violate any restrictions, and (iii) if the new solution is better than the previous, update the best solution.

Results and Discussion

The proposed approach was implemented on a real LV microgrid from Romania where the five PV panels (as SSRES) must be connected, and for which the local generation profiles are considered in the 06:00 – 18:00 interval, values that can be checked in Neagu et al., (2020c). Its one-line diagram is drawn in Figure 5. The µG has a simple structure, with 2 radial feeders and 28 buses, and supplies a number of 27 residences, with one consumer for each pole as is presented in Neagu et al., (2020a). The optimization algorithm (1) – (5) is applied to minimize the power losses for a summer working day. In the initial condition considered, the PV panels is not connected – the daily losses are 149.25 kWh.

The optimal solution is presented in Figure 5. Thus, the consumers located in buses 6, 7, 15, 21, 27 became prosumers trough the connection of the five

PV panels. The buses where prosumers are present are depicted with blue light on the house roof. The objective function for the optimal case (Scenario 0), when all PV panels are connected to the microgrid, was about 96.92 kWh.

In order to carry out a deeper analysis regarding the impact of prosumers operation on microgrid power losses, four scenarios were considered, namely: Scenario 1 (only one prosumer is connected – five cases), Scenario 2 (two prosumers are connected simultaneously – ten cases), Scenario 3 (three prosumers are connected simultaneously - ten cases), and Scenario 4 (four prosumers are connected simultaneously –five cases). All of the proposed scenarios are reported to the initial case and the optimal scenario (Scenarios 0). For instance, the daily energy losses in the Scenario 1 are depicted in Figure 6.

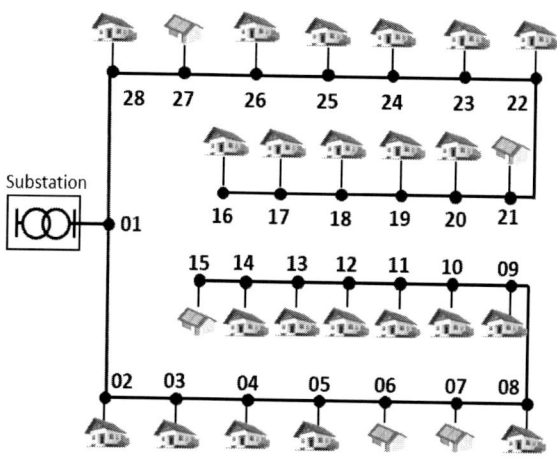

Figure 5. The diagram of the tested LV microgrid.

The minimum value of the losses is obtained in the case when only the prosumer no. 15 is in operation. The reduction is 20.23% compared to the reference case. In the second scenario, there are ten cases as is shown in Figure 7. The minimum value of losses is obtained if the prosumers 7 and 15 are in operation, with a reduction of the daily energy losses of 26.07% compared to the reference case. For the last two Scenarios, the results are indicated in Figures 8 and 9. In Scenario 3 the minimum value of losses is obtained if the prosumers 7, 15 and 21 are in operation on the network, lower by 30.71% compared to the reference case, while in Scenario 4 the energy losses is reduced to 34.37% (the Pros. 27 is not in operation), significantly close to the optimal scenario (35.06%).

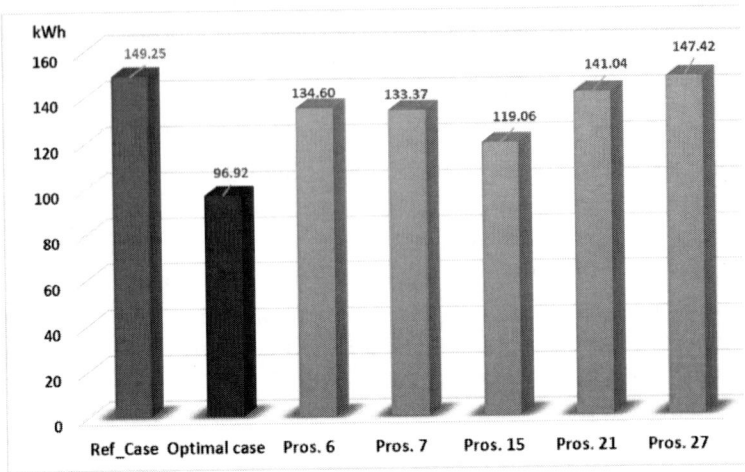

Figure 6. The microgrid daily active energy losses in Scenario 1.

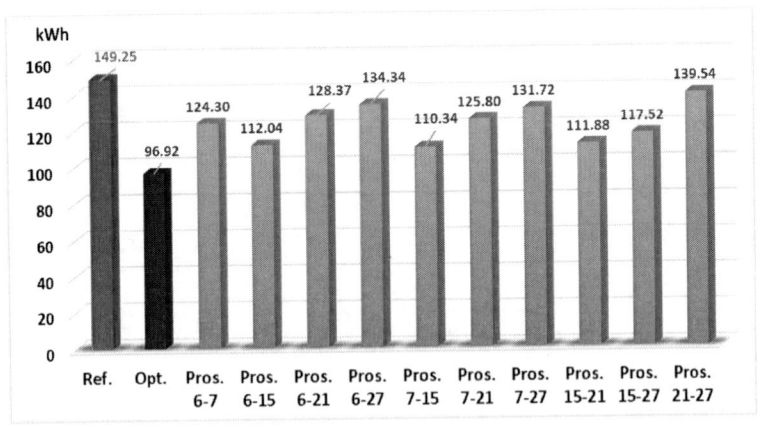

Figure 7. The microgrid daily active energy losses in Scenario 2.

In the most favourable case (Scenario 0 - all prosumers are in operation), the total amount of energy produced by the PV panels in daylight time (06.00-18.00) is 201.03 kWh. If to this quantity the 52.33 kWh (the daily reduced values trough active energy losses) is added, results in a decrease of the amount of energy extracted from the distribution network of 253.36 kWh.

This value is found as technological losses of the network operator as declared in the literature, Neagu et al., (2020d).

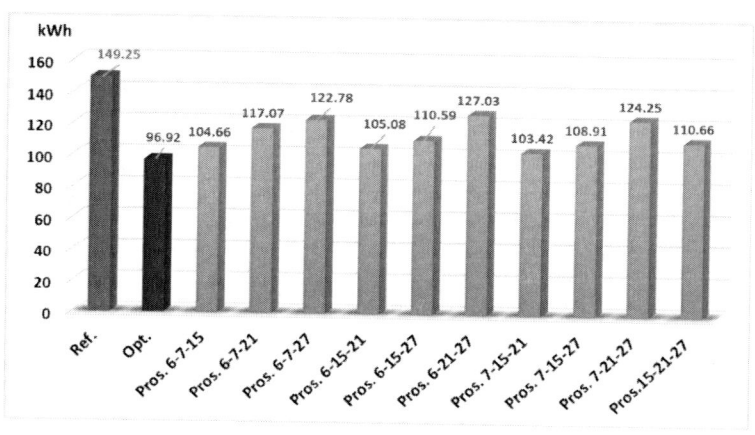

Figure 8. The microgrid daily active energy losses in Scenario 3.

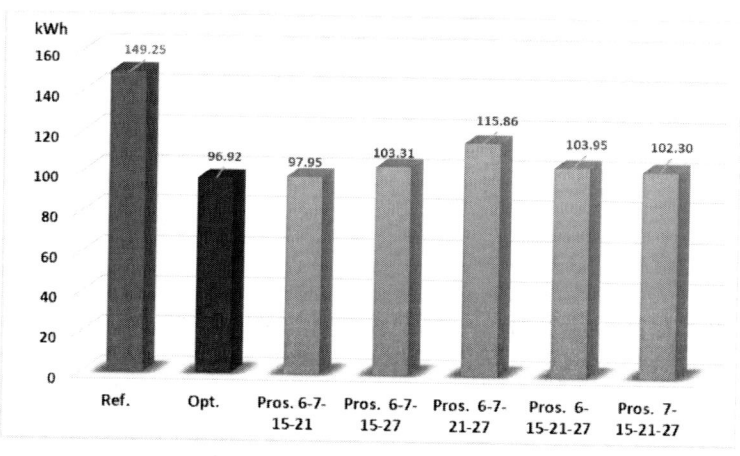

Figure 9. The microgrid daily active energy losses in Scenario 4.

Technically, in the microgrids, prosumers would inject the surplus locally, and the consumers would draw power in the same manner upon the power flow laws. The results emphasize that the DNOs win through optimal electricity flows between the prosumers, and the consumers with high power demand. More than that, the prosumers, located as optimal case at buses 6, 7, 15, 21, and 27, can sell their electricity surplus only to the stakeholders Neagu et al., (2020d).

Conclusion

This research examined a particular approach for optimal placement of small-scale renewable electricity sources for microgrids. Traditionally, local generation helps reduce the network losses. The modern concept of low voltage microgrids, characterized by bidirectional power flow at the level of the same consumer connection allows major changes in the operating techniques of passive (classic) networks that become active distribution networks. At this point, can talk about new types of end user, who are generally more aware and more demanding, more active and more involved. The prosumers form the active cells of the microgrids in which any cell can supply installations to the DNO to optimize the capacity of grid hosting and hence SSRES implementation in a profitable and efficient operating way. In this context, the chapter highlights the obvious capabilities and benefits of integrating prosumers in local microgrids according to the new legislation in our country, to which are added the technical advantages, reduction of energy losses (35.06% for the optimal scenario) by changing the active and reactive powers flow in the microgrid using the crowdsourcing concept and data mining approach. Furthermore, these profiles characterize the prosumers' behaviour from the month with the maximum injected active energy. Based on these approaches the DNO can develop optimal strategies to improve the decision-making process regarding mainly the voltage control and phase load balancing measures. The authors work now on the improvement of this methodology to integrate all prosumers' categories having various generation systems (biomass, wind, hydro, biogas, and geothermal).

References

Alt, F., Shirazi, A. S., Schmidt, A., Kramer, U., and Nawaz, Z., (2010). Location-based crowdsourcing: extending crowdsourcing to the real world. *6th Nordic Conference on Human-Computer Interaction: Extending Boundaries*, 13–22.

Andoni, M., Robu, V., Flynn, D., Abram, S., Geach, D., Jenkins, D., McCallum, P., and Peacock, A., (2010). Blockchain technology in the energy sector: A systematic review of challenges and opportunities, *Renewable and Sustainable Energy Reviews*, 143-174.

Chicco, G., Labate, D., Notaristefano, A., and Piglione, F., (2020). Unveil the Shape: Data Analytics for Extracting Knowledge from Smart Meters, *Energia Elettrica Supplement Journal*, 1-16.

Deng, S., Huang, L., Taheri, J., Yin, J., Zhou, M., and Zomaya, A. Y., (2017). Mobility-Aware Service Composition in Mobile Communities, *IEEE Transactions on Systems, Man, and Cybernetics: Systems*, 555–568.

Diahovchenko, I., Kolcun, M., Čonka, Z., Savkiv, V., and Mykhailyshyn, R., (2020). Progress and Challenges in Smart Grids: Distributed Generation, Smart Metering, Energy Storage and Smart Loads. *Iran Journal Science Technology Transmission Electrical Engineering*, 1-15.

Espe, E., Potdar, V., and Chang, E., (2018). Prosumer Communities and Relationships in Smart Grids: A Literature Review, Evolution and Future Directions. *Energies*, 2528.

European Smart Grids Task Force - Expert Group 3, *Demand Side Flexibility - Perceived barriers and proposed recommendations, Final Report*, Apr. 2019.

Howe, J., (2006). The rise of crowdsourcing. *Wired magazine*, 1–4.

Kazmi, S. A. A., Shahzad, M. K., Khan, A. Z., and Shin, D. R., (2017). Smart Distribution Networks: A Review of Modern Distribution Concepts from a Planning Perspective. *Energies*, 501.

Maxim, A., Mihai, C., Apostoaie, C.-M., Popescu, C., Istrate, C., and Bostan, I., (2016). Implications and Measurement of Energy Poverty across the European Union. *Sustainability*, 483.

Mika, B., and Goudz, A., (2020). Blockchain-technology in the energy industry: blockchain as a driver of the energy revolution? With focus on the situation in Germany. *Energy Systems*.

National Regulatory Authority for Energy. The 228 Order for the Approval of the Technical Norm Technical Conditions for Connection to the Public Electrical Networks of the Prosumers; *National Regulatory Authority for Energy*: Bucharest, Romania, 2018.

Neagu B. C., and Grigoras, G., (2020a). A Fair Load Sharing Approach Based on Microgrid Clusters and Transactive Energy Concept, *12nd Int. Conf. Electr. Comp. and Artif. Intell.*, Bucharest, Romania, 1-4.

Neagu B. C., and Grigoras, G., (2020b). A Data-Mining-Based Methodology to Identify the Behavioural Characteristics of Prosumers within Active Distribution Networks, *International Symposium on Fundamentals of Electrical Engineering 2020* (ISFEE), Bucharest, Romania, 1-4.

Neagu, B. C., Ivanov, O., Grigoras, G., and Gavrilas, M., (2020c). A New Vision on the Prosumers Energy Surplus Trading Considering Smart Peer-to-Peer Contracts. *Mathematics*, 235.

Neagu, B.-C., Ivanov, O., Grigoras, G., Gavrilas, M., and Istrate, D.-M. (2020d). New Market Model with Social and Commercial Tiers for Improved Prosumer Trading in Microgrids. *Sustainability*, 7265.

Neagu, B. C., Grigoras, G., Ivanov, O., (2019). An Efficient Peer-to-Peer Based Blokchain Approach for Prosumers Energy Trading in Microgrids. *International Conference on Modern Power Systems (MPS)*, Cluj Napoca, Romania, 1-4.

Piccinini, E., Gregory, R. W., and Kolbe, L. M., (2015). Changes in the producer-consumer relationship-towards digital transformation. *Changes*, 1634-1648.

Surowiecki, J., (2005). The Wisdom of Crowds; *Anchor*: San Diego, CA, USA.

The Romanian Parliament, "Law no. 184/2018 for approving the Government Emergency Ordinance no. 24/2017 regarding the modification and updating of Law no. 220/2008 for determining the incentive system for producing energy from renewable energy sources and the modification of other normative acts," *Official Gazette*, Part I, No. 635/20.07.2018.

Unguru, M., (2018). Blockchain technology: opportunities for the energy sector, *EUROINFO*, 53-58.

Wang, S., Taha, A. F., Wang, J., Kvaternik, K., and Hahn, A., (2019), Energy Crowdsourcing and Peer-to-Peer Energy Trading in Blockchain-Enabled Smart Grids. *IEEE Transactions on Systems, Man, and Cybernetics: Systems*, 1612–1623.

Chapter 6

Active Learning

Jože M. Rožanec[1,2,3,*], Blaž Fortuna[2] and Dunja Mladenić[1]

[1]Laboratory of Artificial Intelligence, Jožef Stefan Institute, Ljubljana, Slovenia
[2]Qlector d.o.o., Ljubljana, Slovenia
[3]Jožef Stefan International Postgraduate School, Ljubljana, Slovenia

Abstract

Active learning is a sub-field of machine learning concerned with how an active learner can make decisions to draw a limited amount of data instances to minimize the generalization error. The increasing digitalization and growing abundance of data make the active learning approach more critical than ever, introducing new challenges across various disciplines. In the chapter, we introduce the field of active learning, recent advances in the field and provide an overview of relevant use cases across several disciplines.

Keywords: active learning, manufacturing, robotics, learning from demonstration, healthcare

Introduction

Artificial Intelligence is a field of science devoted to learning principles, techniques, and their application to leverage computers and machines to mimic intelligent beings' problem-solving and decision-making capabilities.

---

[*] Corresponding Author's Email: joze.rozanec@ijs.si.

In: The Future of Data Mining
Editor: Cem Ufuk Baytar
ISBN: 979-8-88697-250-4
© 2022 Nova Science Publishers, Inc.

Machine Learning is a sub-field of Artificial Intelligence that focuses on learning such behaviors directly from the data through algorithms. It is thus important that (i) the data is informative towards the goal the model aims to achieve, (ii) the algorithm was suitably chosen to learn how to achieve the goal, and (iii) that the model can learn from the data to achieve the goal. Assuming that (ii) and (iii) were properly resolved and remain constant, the models' performance will depend on how informative the data is: the more informative the data is, the higher the amount of content that can be learned (Seung et al., 1992). Most machine learning algorithms are passive in the sense that they are applied on a randomly selected dataset. Active learning, on the other hand, attempts to influence how relevant instances are selected and therefore impact the machine learning models' learning over time (Tong and Chang, 2001).

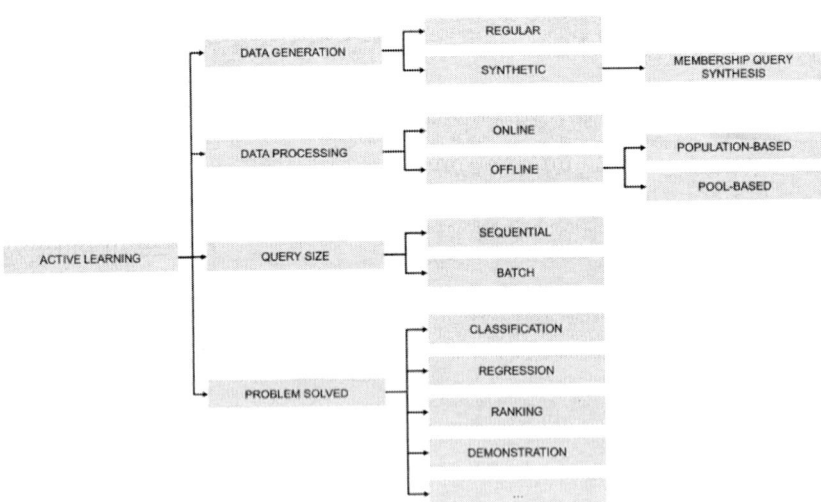

Figure 1. Taxonomy of active learning approaches. Active learning approaches can be divided at least regarding four criteria: (a) how data is generated, (b) how data is processed, (c) the size of the queries posed to the oracle, and (d) the problem solved.

Active Learning approaches and techniques can be characterized at least according to four criteria as shown in Figure 1: (a) how the data is generated, (b) how data is processed, (c) how many instances are queried at a time, and (d) what machine learning problem is being solved. These four characteristics determine the active learning approach. Membership querying synthesis is an active learning approach that attempts to generate synthetic data to be later labeled by an oracle. The challenge with such an approach is to create instances that resemble the real-world data while introducing characteristics that maximize the model's learning. Approaches to select instances face different constraints whether the data is processed in a streaming fashion (an immediate decision must be taken, and memory constraints apply) or the data can be processed offline. Instance selection for persistent data can be classified into two categories (Wu, 2019): population-based (the test distribution is known, and we aim to find the optimal training input density to generate the train samples) and pool-based (select among unlabeled instances for labeling). According to the number of instances queried in each iteration, we can divide the approaches into sequential active learning (single instance) or batch active learning (multiple instances) (Cai et al., 2017). Finally, the active learning approaches differ based on the type of problem they solve (e.g., classification, regression, ranking, and others) and how (e.g., supervised vs. unsupervised) (Kai et al., 2006; Li et al., 2020).

We find supervised machine learning among machine learning approaches, where algorithms are used to learn the mapping between input feature values and their expected outcome. In such settings, active learning is based on the premises that (i) unlabeled data is abundant, (ii) data labeling is expensive, and (iii) the models' generalization error can be minimized by carefully selecting new input instances with which the model is trained (Kruk et al., 2017; Sugiyama and Kawanabe, 2013). The assumption (iii) is grounded on the consideration that the model's bias is small enough to be ignored and that the generalization error can thus be minimized by selecting the data used to train the model. To that end, strategies and criteria were developed to find the best-unlabeled instances to achieve such a purpose. Such a goal can be achieved by selecting them from existing data (in a batch or streaming setting) or generating them. When an unlabeled data instance is obtained, the active learner can query the target value by requesting it to an oracle. The oracle can be anyone or anything (e.g., an application programming interface or a human annotator) that can accurately estimate the target value given the input feature values. While Active Learning can be applied to regression and classification problems, the former has received wider attention in the scientific community.

A supervised Active Learning setting comprehends two distinctive elements: (a) means to obtain some useful, unlabeled data instance (a.k.a. query since we are asking for a label); and (b) an oracle (e.g., a human data annotator) that can provide a label for the aforementioned data instance. The resulting labeled data instance is then used to train the machine learning model, either immediately (in a streaming scenario) or upon model retraining (in a batch scenario, after incorporating it into the labeled dataset). We depict the aforementioned elements in Figure 2. Three aspects must be considered when looking for the most valuable samples (Wu, 2019): informativeness (contains rich information that would benefit the objective function), representativeness (how many other samples are similar to it), and diversity (the samples do not concentrate in a particular region, but rather are scattered across the whole space).

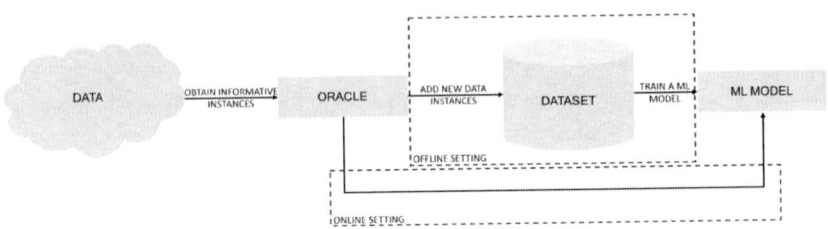

Figure 2. Schematic diagram of active learning. The oracle provides the data directly to the ML model in an online setting. In contrast, in an offline setting, such instances are persisted into a dataset so that the model can leverage them when retrained. The diagram holds for most cases. An exception could be an oracle being directly asked for a particular kind of demonstration, and therefore data selection would not be needed.

In this chapter, we focus mainly on supervised active learning for classification and regression. In section 2, we describe query strategies, mainly for supervised active learning problems, while in section 3, we describe how active learning was applied in use cases related to manufacturing, medicine, and cybersecurity. Finally, we provide our conclusions in section 4.

Query Strategies

A frequent real-world scenario is the availability of large amounts of unlabeled data, from which samples are drawn to create a dataset for supervised learning purposes. Multiple approaches have been devised to that end, some of which we describe. A simple baseline for selecting instances is the Random Active Learning (RAL), which proceeds in rounds and, in each round, randomly samples unlabeled data instances, assuming the data follows a uniform distribution. Cuong, Lee, and Ye (2014) studied greedy active learning criteria in pool-based active learning in a Bayesian setting. They compared the maximum entropy criterion (selects the sample with the highest entropy)

(Settles, 2010), the least confidence criterion (selects the sample whose most probable label has the least probability value) (Lewis, 1995), and the Gibbs error criterion (selects the sample with the largest Gibbs error, which measures the expected error of a Gibbs classifier predicting the label by sampling the current label distribution) (Nguyen et al., 2013). Furthermore, they introduced two greedy algorithms (Hamming loss and F1 loss), which achieved the best performance under worst-case and average-case scenarios.

One of the most popular approaches is the query-by-committee (QBC) framework (Seung et al., 1992), based on the idea that given a committee of machine learning models, the committee's variance can be indirectly measured by examining the disagreement between their predictions. Therefore, candidate data instances among the pool of unlabeled data are selected based on the committee's disagreement. Furthermore, multiple strategies were proposed to measure such disagreement; e.g., Dagan et al. (1993) proposed measuring disagreement using the vote entropy, considering only the final class label regardless of the prediction scores. A variation to the approach mentioned above is to measure the vote entropy by considering the prediction scores of each committee member instead of the predicted labels. Furthermore, a more sophisticated approach would consider measuring the confidence of the committee members by measuring their divergence to the mean and taking into account the class distribution of each committee member (Kee et al., 2018).

Another approach is to consider the disagreement margin, which measures how unanimous the committee is about the given prediction. Abe and Mamitsuka (1998) proposed measuring the disagreement margin by considering the difference of votes between the first and second most confident label estimates for a given instance. Weigl et al., (2016) reframed the aforementioned approach by considering the prediction scores. Another approach was proposed by Borisov et al., (2011), who determined the disagreement based on the standard deviation of the weighted prediction scores of each committee member. Mccallum (1998) modified the QBC approach using Expectation-Maximization to model the density over the unlabeled data instances and use it to weight the disagreement scores to select the unlabeled instances of interest to submit to the oracle.

Gammelsæter (2015) explored a different approach to QBC for neural networks by applying a dropout layer to a Multi-Layer Perceptron (MLP) to form a committee. Nevertheless, adding only one sample per time created an unbalanced weight among the training samples. This issue was addressed by Ducoffe and Precioso (2015), who described a QBC technique to train a convolutional neural network (CNN), leveraging batchwise dropout to create a committee of partial networks given a full network trained by backpropagation. The approach achieved a fast convergence rate and similar error rates by using only 30% of the data available compared to an architecture trained without the active learning approach and on the whole dataset.

While most active learning approaches consider the instance selection and the model's learning as separate tasks, Zhu et al., (2019) proposed considered optimizing both objectives at once. The authors proposed a novel method for QBC active learning of linear models referred to as Robust Zero-Sum Game (RZSG) framework. The authors formulated the sample selection as a robust optimization problem to find the best weights for unlabeled data to minimize the true risk, minimize the average loss (increases robustness to outliers) and minimize the maximal loss (increases robustness to imbalanced data distributions). They compared this approach against another five methods for data selection: (a) random sampling (sampling uniformly at random), (b) a support vector machine margin-based querying technique for incorporating a diversity of selected samples (Brinker, 2003), (c) a variance-based regularization with convex objectives approach, which provides a theoretical performance of the estimator with fast convergence by automatically balancing bias and variance (Duchi and Namkoong, 2019), (d) an approach based on Fisher Information matrices to select a batch of unlabeled samples while reducing the redundancy between them (Zhang and Oles, 2000), and (e) Batch Mode active leaning with Discriminative and Representative queries, which attempts to balance informative and representative samples based on the number of labeled samples (Wang and Ye, 2015). The authors showed that the RZSG method leads to superior results while robust to imbalanced data distribution and outliers and avoids sampling bias.

Searching instances close to the decision boundary has been frequently realized with Support Vector Machine (SVM) models. Cohn and Schohn (2000) described a simple heuristic to enhance the generalization behavior of SVMs on classification tasks. They searched data samples orthogonal to the space spanned by the training set, providing the learner with information about dimensions not yet explored. They also envisioned picking examples along the dividing hyperplane, narrowing the existing margin, and improving the confidence in the dimensions the model already has information about. In the same line, Tong and Chang (2001) proposed using uncertainty sampling for an SVM model, querying the unlabeled data instances whose projection is closest to the SVM hyperplane. Martens, Baesens and Gestel (2009), on the other side, developed the Active Learning-Based Approach (ALBA) that extracts rules from an SVM model to gain insight into its rationale and then uses active learning to enhance the discrimination rules close to the SVM decision boundary. A different take on the problem was developed by Guo and Greiner (2007), who proposed querying unlabeled data instances, selecting those providing the maximum conditional mutual information given the labeled data, and using an optimistic guess for the unlabeled instances. There are two possible scenarios given the optimistic guess: either the guess was correct or not.

When the guess is incorrect, the authors propose selecting the most uncertain unlabeled data instance, which helps to clarify the model's decision boundary. In the same line, Beygelzimer, Dasgupta and Langford (2009) introduced the Importance Weighted Active Learning (IWAL), advocating the relevance of importance weights to ensure a correct sampling bias. The learner uses a specific strategy to estimate a rejection probability threshold based on the unlabeled data instance and history of unlabeled samples queried to the oracle. The weight of the particular instance is determined as the inverse of the rejection probability, and used only if such data instance is queried against the oracle. Another method for weighting instances was developed by Ganti and Gray (2012), who devised the Unbiased Pool Based Active Learning (UPAL) algorithm for pool-based active learning. The algorithm proceeds in rounds, putting a probability distribution over the entire pool to then sample a point from the pool. The probability distribution in each round depends on the active learner and is obtained by minimizing the importance of weighted risk over the hypothesis space. The authors demonstrated that UPAL outperforms the Batch Mode Active Learning (BMAL) algorithm Hoi et al., (2006) in terms of discriminative power, scalability, and execution time.

Xu et al., (2003) developed an approach to take into account the diversity of data samples. To that end, the authors performed representative sampling by clustering unlabeled data instances close to the decision boundary of an SVM model and then selecting the medoid instances, which are expected to preserve the density distribution information of the whole cluster. A similar approach was followed by Nguyen and Smeulders (2004), who proposed using clustering over all unlabeled data and then finding candidate samples considering unlabeled data instances close to the decision boundary and medoids of the highest density clusters. The one that contributes most to the current error is chosen from the initial set of candidates. The authors argue that while such a choice does not guarantee to achieve the smallest future error, it is highly probable that such a choice would lead to a significant error decrease.

Yang, Hanneke and Carbonell (2013) explored the use of active learning in a transfer learning setting, where target concepts are sampled from an unknown distribution. Furthermore, the authors explored the benefits of transfer learning to know whether to stop the active learning procedure (self-verifying active learning). In their research, they contrasted their work with research from Baxter (1997) regarding the role of the sample size and loss observed in learning multiple tasks. Yang, Hanneke and Carbonell (2013) consider that the results are related only to the number of tasks. In contrast, the number of samples per task remains bounded given non-altruistic learners and the fact that the desired number of labeled samples should never be significantly larger than the number of samples required to solve the task. The authors consider that transfer learning can be used in a setting where all problems cannot be solved by a single individual but rather by a coalition of cooperating individuals who are willing to share the data used to learn a particular concept to help others to learn another task. Furthermore, they demonstrate that transfer learning can lead to a sample complexity close to the one achieved by algorithms that directly know the targets' distribution. Shao (2019) also addressed the problem of actively selecting informative instances aided by transferred knowledge from related tasks. To that end, the authors proposed using a diverse committee with members from both domains to select the most informative instances based on the maximum vote entropy, improve the classification accuracy and evaluate each member over multiple iterations.

A whole different view of the active learning problem was developed by Zhu, Ghahramani and Lafferty (2003), who envisioned combining semi-supervised learning and Active Learning by transforming labeled and unlabeled data into vertices of a weighted graph connected by edges indicating the similarity between data instances. While the semi-supervised learning problem was framed in terms of a Gaussian random field model on the graph, active learning was used to query unlabeled data and minimize the expected classification error of the semi-supervised model. Active learning was also applied to graph-specific problems. Ma, Garnett and Schneider (2013) developed a graph-specific criterion called Σ-optimality, querying the nodes that minimize the sum of the elements in the predictive covariance. Ostapuk, Yang and Cudré-Mauroux (2019) developed an active learning framework for knowledge graphs that takes into account the model uncertainty and the underlying structure of the knowledge graph to improve the sampling effectiveness and incrementally train deep learning models. A different approach was developed by Li, Yin and Chen (2021), who proposed a

SEmisupervised Adversarial active Learning (SEAL) framework on attributed graphs. The framework learns two adversarial components: (a) a graph embedding network to encode labeled and unlabeled nodes into a common latent space and (b) a semi-supervised discriminator network that learns to distinguish between labeled and unlabeled nodes. The most informative instances are then selected based on a divergence score generated by the discriminator and submitted to an oracle for labeling.

Active learning has been successfully applied to regression problems too. Wu (2019) considers three criteria must be taken into account when selecting unlabeled samples: informativeness (the information richness of the samples, which positively affects the objective function), representativeness (the density of samples close to a certain target sample), and diversity (ensures the samples are scattered across the full input space). The authors compare four techniques: QBC, Expected Model Change Maximization (EMCM) Cai, Zhang and Zhou (2013), Enhanced Batch Mode Active Learning for Regression (EBMALR) (Wu et al., 2016) and greedy sampling (GS) (Yu and Kim 2010). EMCM uses a set of labeled examples to create a linear regression model M1 and then uses bootstrap to build a set of linear regression models whose predictions are compared against the ones of M1 for a set of unlabeled instances. To select the unlabeled instances, the algorithm considers those with the maximum value given the average of the difference between predictions of the M1 model and the set of linear regressors. EBMALR simultaneously considers the informativeness, representativeness, and diversity of samples, enhancing the QBC and EMCM approaches. To that end, it uses k-means clustering to initialize a set of representative and diverse samples and then recurs to baseline techniques to select subsequent samples sequentially. Finally, greedy sampling attempts to find the most informative sample based on the geometric characteristics of the feature space, selecting new samples that are located far away from the previously selected and labeled samples.

The abovementioned methods described different strategies to select existing data suitable for streaming and batch processing. The membership query synthesis active learning strategy considers no data is selected, but rather a data instance is created and presented to the oracle. J.-J. Zhu and Bento (2017) introduced the Generative Adversarial Active Learning (GAAL) technique, which leverages Generative Adversarial Networks (GANs) to generate informative instances based on a random sample of unlabeled instances close to the decision boundary. Mahapatra et al. (2018) evolved this concept by generating synthetic data with a conditional GAN, which learns to create a specific instance leveraging additional data regarding the desired target label and therefore leading to faster convergence. Sinha, Ebrahimi, and Darrell (2019) introduced the variational adversarial active learning, sampling instances using an adversarially trained discriminator to predict whether the instance is labeled or not based on the latent space of the variational auto-encoder. A weakness of this approach is that it can end up selecting instances that correspond to the same class, regardless of the proportion of labeled samples per class. This issue was addressed by Laielli et al. (2020), who developed a semi-supervised mini-max entropy-based active learning algorithm that leverages uncertainty and diversity in an adversarial manner. A similar approach was described by Liu et al. (2019), who proposed the Single-Objective Generative Adversarial Active Learning (SO-GAAL) technique, which generates outliers with informative potential based on the mini-max game between a generator and a discriminator to assist a classifier on describing a boundary that separates outliers from normal data.

The overview of query methods provided above is by no means exhaustive. We refer the reader to the following surveys to learn more about active learning in particular settings. The surveys by Fu, Zhu and Li (2013), and Kumar and Gupta (2020) provide great insights about query strategies for classification, regression, and clustering in a batch setting. To learn about techniques applied with deep learning models, we recommend the survey by Ren et al. (2021). Finally, the survey by Lughofer (2017) provides an in-depth introduction to active learning in an online setting.

Use Case

Industry and Robotics

While there is currently a research void regarding the use of active learning in the manufacturing domain (Meng et al., 2020), the increasing digitalization makes such approaches ever more relevant. Active learning has been recognized to alleviate the manual labeling workload. Such quality has been exploited in the manufacturing setting too. Furthermore, active learning is considered one of the pillars of human-machine collaboration, key to the Industry 5.0 paradigm (Rožanec et al., 2022a).

It can be argued that the manufacturing process begins with acquiring the raw material and components required to manufacture the product. Accurate demand forecasting is key to avoiding distortions across the supply chain.

Machine learning has been demonstrated to provide accurate forecasts (Rožanec et al., 2021). In addition, explainable artificial intelligence methods provide insights into the reasons behind such a forecast to craft explanations and enable responsible decision-making (Rožanec et al., 2022b; Rožanec et al., 2022c). Such explanations can be enriched with data from external sources, recommending relevant pieces of data. In this line, Zajec et al., (2021) explored different active learning strategies to combine recommendations and active learning when displaying entries in such explanations so that the entries were accurate and interesting to the user while relevant to the model's learning process. In a similar line of research, Li et al., (2017) developed a machine learning model to assess whether input components required for the manufacturing of fiber optic components will be delivered on time. The manufacturing firm had valuable information to guide decision-making to mitigate such risk by accurately predicting delayed customer orders. The authors used active learning to select and label the most valuable samples that are believed to maximize the classifier's performance.

In manufacturing, significant resources are invested in qualifying processes and machines that conform to quality and productivity standards. One of such qualification procedures can be using experimental methods to find the response surface mapping to process parameters. Botcha et al., (2021) proposed using QBC-based active learning to find the next best experimental point to reduce the uncertainty of prediction of surface roughness over the sample space and avoid testing all possible parameters.

Active learning has been successfully applied to many quality inspection use cases. Garderen (2017) explored its use in the quality process of measuring the local displacement between layers on a chip, given that the ability to limit overlay is key to the quality of semiconductor chips manufactured at a nanometer scale. Quality measurements are performed in a separate metrology tool. Since they are difficult to perform and time-consuming, only a fraction of the produced wafers are analyzed. The authors compared several methods which would be suitable for a regression problem that enabled forecasting and visualization. Among the considerations they raised are that active learning skews the sampling distribution, the results may have limited generalization since selection results can vary across datasets, and that the sampling bias that has been effective for a particular model does not provide performance guarantees for others. In the same industry, Shim et al., (2020) describes how wafer maps provide key information to engineers to detect root causes of failure in the semiconductor manufacturing process. While a SOTA machine learning model was built to classify them, a considerable cost is required to gather enough labeled data samples. The authors described an active learning approach to select the wafer maps to alleviate this issue, ensuring no effort is invested into data samples that would not provide enough information to the classifier to learn. Dai et al., (2018) described a use case regarding automatic optical inspection for the recognition of solder joint defects in printed circuit boards. Active learning is applied to enlarge an initially labeled dataset. The authors developed an original method combining semi-supervised learning and active learning. In particular, they performed k-means clustering on labeled and unlabeled data and trained a classifier on labeled data. They later used the predictions issued by the classifier to analyze which clusters had the least skewed distributions when considering the predicted classes of the unlabeled samples and sample unlabeled data from them. A different use case for visual inspection was described by Rožanec et al., (2022d); Trajkova et al., (2021), where multiple active learning approaches were considered to reduce the manual visual inspection and labeling effort when inspecting the quality of printed logos on manufactured shavers.

Active learning addresses the problem of which data to request to the oracle to maximize the learning of a given agent. This idea strongly connects with research on how robots are taught from human demonstrations and how a physical robot can improve its skills by asking for such demonstrations. For example, Maeda et al., (2017) describes an active learning approach that enables robots to decide whether they have the skill to deal with an unknown task or must ask for demonstrations to learn movement primitives incrementally. In the same line of research, Conkey and Hermans (2019) explored the use of active learning to learn a library of probabilistic movement primitives, while Koert et al., (2019) used active learning to rely on fewer demonstrations while improving the generalization capabilities when learning a specific set of tasks. For a more in-depth overview of the use of active learning in robotics, we refer the reader to the survey by Taylor, Berrueta, and Murphey (2021).

Healthcare

Artificial intelligence can bring virtually unlimited progress to the field of healthcare. One of the problems to which it has been successfully applied is to annotate and help determine whether a patient suffers from a certain illness or not. Much research was performed in the field of radiomics to perform such analysis based on medical images. One such example is work by Doyle et al.,

(2011), who used weak decision tree classifiers to determine carcinoma and non-carcinoma regions on prostate histopathological images. The authors used a QBC active learning to annotate the images with the highest discrepancy between the classification trees in a bagging setting. Padmanabhan et al., (2014) used artificial intelligence to detect and analyze the chemical and physical characteristics of human cells in the context of renal carcinoma detection. The authors reported using active learning to quantify the information contribution of unlabeled samples by estimating the determinant of the Fisher information matrix. The samples expected to provide the greatest contribution were selected for manual labeling. Das, Nair, and Peter (2020) described the use of artificial intelligence to analyze histopathological tissue sample images and determine variations in size and shape that correspond to malignant lesions associated with breast cancer. Given that the annotation of such images requires a considerable effort of domain experts and experienced pathologists, the authors used Active Learning to select batches of instances based on the kernelized Riemannian distance measures, such as the Jeffrey and Stein divergences. Among the results, they report using only 20% of the labeled data required to train a supervised classifier model without the active learning setting. A different approach was developed by Doyle and Madabhushi (2010), who used a consensus of ambiguity to identify images considered ambiguous by multiple algorithms and prioritize them for manual labeling. Active learning has been also successfully applied to image classification models related to the detection of colorectal cancer (Zhao et al., 2019), skin lesions (Shi et al., 2019) or other diseases, such as COVID-19 or pneumonia (Wu et al., 2021; Nguyen et al., 2021).

Accurate diagnostics require the right level of medical expertise to assess the evidence. Mu et al., (2021) reported using deep learning to map semi-structured and unstructured text data from pathology synopses to provide relevant semantic diagnostic labels. Such a system attempts to avoid bottlenecks that result from the limited number of specialists available to interpret the pathology synopses and provide relevant diagnostic information. In addition, the authors used active learning to prioritize the labeling of unlabeled samples considering those that are underrepresented in the dataset or the ones that could enhance the models' performance.

Once a disease is discovered, it is crucial to understand how critical it is to ensure the best treatment possible for the patient while also meeting the overall patient scheduling constraints. This problem was addressed by Nissim et al., (2017), who developed the CAESAR-ALE (Classification Approach for Extracting Severity Automatically from Electronic Health Records - Active

Learning Enhancement) framework to determine the urgency of further diagnoses and the seniority of personnel required to attend to such patients. The authors reported using an SVM classifier to classify the clinical records and leverage active learning to reduce the labeling effort between 48% to 64% compared to a standard passive SVM model.

Active learning has also been successfully applied to guide clinical trials. One such example is research done by Minsker et al., (2016), who explored the usage of artificial intelligence to optimize the selection of patients for clinical trials to learn the best individual treatment rules. The authors argue that randomized clinical trials are expensive and usually not efficiently designed to estimate the individual treatment rules. Therefore, they use Active Learning to estimate which persons can be considered the most informative patients and let such insights guide further recruitment over the ongoing clinical trials. They exclude the patients on whom the treatment effects are clearly observed and focus on those where further evidence is required, reducing overall sample sizes and associated costs.

Artificial intelligence can also be applied to search for proper treatment and cures. Jin et al., (2020) described how academic papers are retrieved and analyzed to understand reported critical clinical evidence related to a given treatment in populations characterized by a disease and gene mutation. They use Active Learning to leverage expert annotations to enhance a ranking model that considers scores from an information retrieval system, a pre-trained BioBERT model, publication type, and citation counts. The BioBERT model is used for each iteration to propose relevant unannotated query-document instances and then finetuned given the experts' input. A different use case was proposed by Danziger et al., (2009), who used artificial intelligence to determine which mutations result enables the production of proteins with a particular function. In particular, they sought mutations in the tumor suppressor protein p53 since p53 mutants are found in half of all human cancers. Restoring the non-mutant p53 proteins in tumors leads to their decrease. The authors developed a specific active learning strategy (Most Informative Positive) tailored to biological problems to select functionally active examples compatible with further exploration of combinatorial mutagenesis. The above strategy enabled reducing the number of experiments by a third without a significant classification performance decrease.

Cybersecurity

The increasing complexity of cyberspace security requires intelligence-driven cybersecurity defense. Machine learning applications to the cybersecurity domain range from the development and mining of knowledge graphs (to provide intelligence to the security analyst) to detecting and preventing cybersecurity attacks. While the construction of knowledge graphs based on deep learning has achieved great success, it requires the annotation of large corpora. The annotation effort can be alleviated through active learning. One such approach is described by Xie et al., (2021), who combined active learning and deep learning frameworks to recognize and annotate Chinese cybersecurity entities in Chinese texts. To that end, they build upon the work of active learning for entity recognition by Shen et al., (2017), and Chinese cybersecurity entity recognition by Qin et al., (2019) and propose a selection strategy with uncertainty and confidence while considering the lexicon. The authors used a BERT pre-trained model and a residual dilation convolutional neural network to learn entity context features and conditional random fields for tag decoding. They complemented the model with an active learning approach, selecting the highest uncertainty cases computed considering the posterior probability. Given that the method tends to favor long sentences, the authors computed the confidence of the label of the sentence in the decoding process and the matching frequency of cybersecurity entities in a lexicon to evaluate whether the sentence should be sent to manual revision.

The use of active learning to guide manual revision has also been leveraged for other problems. Chung et al., (2020) performed research regarding the monitoring of internal networks to prevent data exfiltrations. The authors developed an active learning approach to complement anomaly detection models with manual revision to deal with the many false alarms and learn from them. To that end, they used a LightGBM classifier and queried unlabeled samples based on their entropy. Nevertheless, the authors observed that while the models' overall performance increases over time, it can lead to the fact that the model can improve its performance for certain classes while degrading others with each retrain. Similarly, Dang (2020) described using active learning in the context of an intrusion detection system to reduce the labeling cost while maintaining the classification performance. They trained a Naive Bayes algorithm and selected rare events detected by the Isolation Forest, which measures the difference of an instance regarding the observed distribution. The decision of whether to include the selected instance into the train set is made based on the predicted performance impact in terms of AUC

ROC change by an ad-hoc XGBoost model. Concept drift can make machine learning models vulnerable to attackers who progressively distill attack traces into models and make them hard to distinguish from the values change related to the concept drift. Dey et al., (2020) explored using active learning to leverage human expertise and maintain effective detection capabilities even in the face of concept drift regarding behavioral models.

Active learning was also used to timely annotate data for other cybersecurity-related problems. Das Bhattacharjee et al., (2017), who describe the use of active learning to create a semi-supervised solution to annotate data regarding Phishing categorization. Among the particular challenges of the domain is the need for real-time detection (the user must be warned about the potential danger before (s)he clicks on the URL) and the ability to generalize beyond the blacklisted URLs. The authors used the uncertainty sampling strategy to achieve greater clarity near the classifier's decision boundaries and increase the model's performance.

Conclusion

The active learning sub-field of machine learning is concerned with finding the right data instances that maximize a given algorithm's learning goal. Through this chapter, we introduced a taxonomy, showing how multiple criteria constrain and influence the development and choice of active learning methods. We then provided a high-level overview of query strategies to select or create relevant data samples and described research on use cases from manufacturing and robotics, healthcare, and cybersecurity.

The decreased cost of sensors and digital devices favors an increasing digitalization of every aspect of our lives. The abundance of collected data and increasing ease of access to it has enabled the development of machine learning models and products addressing a wide range of needs. Furthermore, it has refocused the attention of research back to the quality of data with a particular concern on how it is helpful to solve the particular problem at hand. We consider active learning to play a crucial role in the renewed attention towards data-centric artificial intelligence, developing a new understanding of how to acquire data that drives the best learning outcomes for the algorithms and overall artificial-intelligence-powered solutions.

References

Abe, N., Mamitsuka, H., 1998. Query Learning Strategies Using Boosting and Bagging. In *ICML '98: Proceedings of the Fifteenth International Conference on Machine Learning*, 1–9.

Baxter, J., 1997. A Bayesian/Information Theoretic Model of Learning to Learn via Multiple Task Sampling. *Machine Learning* 28 (1), 7–39. https://doi.org/10.1023/A:100 73 27622663.

Beygelzimer, A., Dasgupta, S., Langford, J., 2009. Importance Weighted Active Learning. *Proceedings of the 26th International Conference On Machine Learning, ICML 2009*, no. 2008, 49–56.

Bhattacharjee, S. D., Talukder, A., Al-Shaer, E., Doshi, P., 2017. Prioritized Active Learning for Malicious URL Detection Using Weighted Text-Based Features. *2017 IEEE International Conference on Intelligence and Security Informatics: Security and Big Data, ISI 2017*, 107–12. https://doi.org/10.1109/ISI.2017.8004883.

Borisov, A., Tuv, E., Runger, G., 2011. Active Batch Learning with Stochastic Query-by-Forest (SQBF). *Workshop on Active Learning and Experimental Design* 16, 59–69.

Botcha, B., Iquebal, A. S., Bukkapatnam, S. B., 2021. Efficient Manufacturing Processes and Performance Qualification via Active Learning: Application to a Cylindrical Plunge Grinding Platform. *Procedia Manufacturing* 53 (2020), 716–725. https://doi.org/10.1016/j.promfg.2021.06.070.

Brinker, K,, 2003. Incorporating Diversity in Active Learning with Support Vector Machines. In *Proceedings of the Twentieth International Conference on Machine Learning (ICML-2003)*. https://doi.org/10.1039/C19680000233.

Cai, W., Muhan Z., Ya Z., 2017. Batch Mode Active Learning for Regression with Expected Model Change. *IEEE Transactions on Neural Networks and Learning Systems* 28 (7), 1668–1681. https://doi.org/10.1109/TNNLS.2016.2542184.

Cai, W., Zhang, Y., Zhou, J., 2013. Maximizing Expected Model Change for Active Learning in Regression. *Proceedings - IEEE International Conference on Data Mining, ICDM*, 51–60. https://doi.org/10.1109/ICDM.2013.104.

Chung, M-H., Chignell, M., Wang, L., Jovicic, A., Raman, A., 2020. Interactive Machine Learning for Data Exfiltration Detection: Active Learning with Human Expertise. *Conference Proceedings - IEEE International Conference on Systems, Man and Cybernetics* 2020-October: 280–287. https://doi.org/10.1109/SMC42975.2020.9282831.

Conkey, A., Hermans, T., 2019. Active Learning of Probabilistic Movement Primitives. *IEEE-RAS International Conference on Humanoid Robots* 2019-October, 425-432. https://doi.org/10.1109/Humanoids43949.2019.9035026.

Cuong, N. V., Lee, W. S., Ye, N., 2014. Near-Optimal Adaptive Pool-Based Active Learning with General Loss. *Uncertainty in Artificial Intelligence - Proceedings of the 30th Conference, UAI 2014*, 122–131.

Dagan, I., Engelson, S. P., and Gan, R., 1993. Committee-Based Sampling For Training Probabilistic Classifiers. *Science*.

Dai, W., Mujeeb, A., Erdt, M., Sourin, A., 2018. Towards Automatic Optical Inspection of Soldering Defects. *Proceedings - 2018 International Conference on Cyberworlds, CW 2018*, 375–382. https://doi.org/10.1109/CW.2018.00074.

Dang, Q. V., 2020. Proceedings - 2020 RIVF International Conference on Computing and Communication Technologies, RIVF 2020. In *2020 RIVF International Conference on Computing and Communication Technologies (RIVF)*, 13.

Danziger, S. A., Baronio, R., Ho, L., Hall, L., Salmon, K., Hatfield, G. W., Kaiser, P., Lathrop, R. H., 2009. Predicting Positive P53 Cancer Rescue Regions Using Most Informative Positive (MIP) Active Learning. *PLoS Computational Biology* 5 (9). https://doi.org/10.1371/journal.pcbi.1000498.

Das, A., Nair, M.S., Peter, D.S., 2020. Batch Mode Active Learning on the Riemannian Manifold for Automated Scoring of Nuclear Pleomorphism in Breast Cancer. *Artificial Intelligence in Medicine* 103, 101805. https://doi.org/10.1016/j.artmed.2020.101805.

Dey, A., Velay, M., Fauvelle, J-P., Navers, S., 2020. *Adversarial vs Behavioural-Based Defensive AI with Joint, Continual and Active Learning: Automated Evaluation of Robustness to Deception, Poisoning and Concept Drift*, 1–25. http://arxiv.org/abs/2001.11821.

Doyle, S., Madabhushi, A., 2010. Consensus of ambiguity: theory and application of active learning for biomedical image analysis. *In IAPR International Conference on Pattern Recognition in Bioinformatics*, 313–324.

Doyle, S., Monaco, J., Feldman, M., Tomaszewski, J., Madabhushi, A., 2011. An Active Learning Based Classification Strategy for the Minority Class Problem: Application to Histopathology Annotation. *BMC Bioinformatics* 12, 1–14. https://doi.org/10.1186/1471-2105-12-424.

Duchi, J., Namkoong H., 2019. Variance-Based Regularization with Convex Objectives. *Journal of Machine Learning Research* 20 (3), 1–10.

Ducoffe, M., Precioso, F., 2015. QBDC: Query by Dropout Committee for Training Deep Supervised Architecture, no. 2013, 1–10. http://arxiv.org/abs/1511.06412.

Fu, Y., Zhu, X., Li, B., 2013. A Survey on Instance Selection for Active Learning. *Knowledge and Information Systems* 35 (2), 249–283. https://doi.org/10.1007/s10115-012-0507-8.

Gammelsæter, M., 2015. *A Committee of One - Using Dropout for Active Learning in Deep Networks* | Semantic Scholar. 2015.

Ganti, R., Gray, A., 2012. UPAL: Unbiased Pool Based Active Learning. *Journal of Machine Learning Research* 22 (422), 422–431.

Garderen, K. V., 2017. Active Learning for Overlay Prediction in Semi-Conductor Manufacturing 6 (0), 1–18.

Guo, Y., Greiner, R., 2007. Optimistic Active Learning Using Mutual Information. *IJCAI International Joint Conference on Artificial Intelligence*, 823–829.

Hoi, S. C. H., Jin, R., Zhu, J., Lyu, M. R., 2006. Batch Mode Active Learning and Its Application to Medical Image Classification. *ACM International Conference Proceeding Series* 148, 417–424. https://doi.org/10.1145/1143844.1143897.

Jin, Q., Tan, C., Chen, M., Yan, M., Huang, S., Zhang, N., Liu, X., 2020. Aliababa DAMO academy at TREC precision medicine 2020: State-of-the-art evidence retriever for precision medicine with expert-in-the-loop active learning. *In Proceedings of the Twenty-Ninth Text REtrieval Conference, TREC,* 16–20.

Kai, Y., Bi, J., Volker, T., 2006. Active Learning via Transductive Experimental Design. *ACM International Conference Proceeding Series* 148, 1081–1088. https://doi.org/10.1145/1143844.1143980.

Kee, S., del Castillo, E., Runger, G., 2018. Query-by-Committee Improvement with Diversity and Density in Batch Active Learning. *Information Sciences* 454, 401–418. https://doi.org/10.1016/j.ins.2018.05.014.

Koert, D., Pajarinen, J., Schotschneider, A., Trick, S., Rothkopf, C., Peters J., 2019. Learning Intention Aware Online Adaptation of Movement Primitives, in *IEEE Robotics and Automation Letters,* 4 (4), 3719-3726.

Kruk, M. E., Emilia, J. L., Asaf, B., Melani, C., Karen, C., Mickey, C., Fadi, E. J., 2017. Building Resilient Health Systems: A Proposal for a Resilience Index. *BMJ (Online).* https://doi.org/10.1136/bmj.j2323.

Kumar, P., Gupta, A., 2020. Active Learning Query Strategies for Classification, Regression, and Clustering: A Survey. *Journal of Computer Science and Technology* 35. https://doi.org/10.1007/s11390-020-9487-4.

Laielli, M., Zhu, S., Darrell. T., 2020. *Minimax active learning.* arXiv preprint arXiv:2012.10467.

Lewis, D. D., 1995. A Sequential Algorithm for Training Text Classifiers. *ACM SIGIR Forum* 29 (2), 13–19. https://doi.org/10.1145/219587.219592.

Li, C., Handong, M., Zhao, K., Ye, Y., Xiao, Y.Z., Guoren, W., 2020. On Deep Unsupervised Active Learning. *IJCAI International Joint Conference on Artificial Intelligence* 2021-Janua, 2626–2632. https://doi.org/10.24963/ijcai.2020/364.

Li, Q., Wei, F., Zhou, S., 2017. Early Warning Systems for Multi-Variety and Small Batch Manufacturing Based on Active Learning. *Journal of Intelligent and Fuzzy Systems* 33 (5), 2945–2952. https://doi.org/10.3233/JIFS-169345.

Li, Y., Yin, J., Chen, L., 2021. SEAL: Semisupervised Adversarial Active Learning on Attributed Graphs. *IEEE Transactions on Neural Networks and Learning Systems* 32 (7), 3136–3147. https://doi.org/10.1109/TNNLS.2020.3009682.

Liu, Y., Li, Z., Zhou, C., Jiang, Y., Sun, J., Wang, M., He, X., 2019. Generative Adversarial Active Learning for Unsupervised Outlier Detection. *IEEE Transactions on Knowledge and Data Engineering* 32 (8), 1517–1528. https://doi.org/10.1109/TKDE.2019.2905606.

Lughofer, E., 2017. On-Line Active Learning: A New Paradigm to Improve Practical Useability of Data Stream Modeling Methods. *Information Sciences* 415–416, 356–376. https://doi.org/10.1016/j.ins.2017.06.038.

Ma, Y., Garnett, R., Schneider, J., 2013. Σ-Optimality for Active Learning on Gaussian Random Fields. *Advances in Neural Information Processing Systems,* 1–9.

Maeda, G., Ewerton, M., Osa, T., Busch, B., Peters, J., 2017. Active Incremental Learning of Robot Movement Primitives. *Conference on Robot Learning (CoRL),* no. CoRL, 37–46.

Mahapatra, D., Bozorgtabar, B., Thiran, J. P., Reyes, M., 2018. Efficient Active Learning for Image Classification and Segmentation Using a Sample Selection and Conditional Generative Adversarial Network. *Lecture Notes in Computer Science (Including*

Subseries Lecture Notes in Artificial Intelligence and Lecture Notes in Bioinformatics) 11071 LNCS, 580–588. https://doi.org/10.1007/978-3-030-00934-2_65.

Martens, D., Baesens, B., Gestel, T. V., 2009. Decompositional Rule Extraction from Support Vector Machines by Active Learning. *IEEE Transactions on Knowledge and Data Engineering* 21 (2), 178–191. https://doi.org/10.1109/TKDE.2008.131.

Mccallum, A., 1998. Employing EM in Pool-Based Active Learning for Text Classification 1 Introduction. *ICML '98: Proceedings of the Fifteenth International Conference on Machine Learning*.

Meng, L., McWilliams, B., Jarosinski, W., Park, H. Y., Jung, Y. G., Lee, J., Zhang, J., 2020. Machine Learning in Additive Manufacturing: A Review. *Jom* 72 (6), 2363–2377. https://doi.org/10.1007/s11837-020-04155-y.

Minsker, S., Zhao, Y. Q., Cheng, G., 2016. Active Clinical Trials for Personalized Medicine. *J Am Stat Assoc.* 176 (3), 139–148. https://doi.org/10.1080/01621459.2015.1066682.Active.

Mu, Y., Tizhoosh, H. R., Tayebi, R. M., Ross, C., Sur, M., Leber, B., Campbell, C. J. V., 2021. A BERT Model Generates Diagnostically Relevant Semantic Embeddings from Pathology Synopses with Active Learning. *Communications Medicine* 1 (1). https://doi.org/10.1038/s43856-021-00008-0.

Nguyen, C. D. T., Huynh, M. T., Tran, M. Q., Nguyen, N. H., Jain, M., Van, D. N., Vo, T.D., Bui, T. H., Truong, S. Q. H., 2021. GOAL: Gist-Set Online Active Learning for Efficient Chest X-Ray Image Annotation. *Proceedings of Machine Learning Research* 143, 545–553.

Nguyen, H. T., Smeulders, A., 2004. Active Learning Using Pre-Clustering. *Proceedings, Twenty-First International Conference on Machine Learning, ICML 2004*, 623–630. https://doi.org/10.1145/1015330.1015349.

Nguyen, V. C., Wee, Sun, L., Nan, Y., Kian, M. A. C., Hai, L. C., 2013. Active Learning for Probabilistic Hypotheses Using the Maximum Gibbs Error Criterion. *Advances in Neural Information Processing Systems*, 1–9.

Nissim, N., Shahar, Y., Elovici, Y., Hripcsak, G., Moskovitch, R., 2017. Inter-Labeler and Intra-Labeler Variability of Condition Severity Classification Models Using Active and Passive Learning Methods. *Artificial Intelligence in Medicine* 81, 12–32. https://doi.org/10.1016/j.artmed.2017.03.003.

Ostapuk, N., Yang, J., Cudré-Mauroux, P., 2019. ActiveLink: Deep Active Learning for Link Prediction in Knowledge Graphs. *The Web Conference 2019 - Proceedings of the World Wide Web Conference, WWW 2019*, 1398–1408. https://doi.org/10.1145/3308558.3313620.

Padmanabhan, R. K., Somasundar, V. H., Griffith, S. D., Zhu, J., Samoyedny, D., Tan, K. S., et al., 2014. An Active Learning Approach for Rapid Characterization of Endothelial Cells in Human Tumors. *PLoS ONE* 9 (3). https://doi.org/10.1371/journal.pone.0090495.

Qin, Y., Shen, G. W., Zhao, W. B., Chen, Y. P., Yu, M., Jin, X., 2019. A Network Security Entity Recognition Method Based on Feature Template and CNN-BiLSTM-CRF. *Frontiers of Information Technology and Electronic Engineering* 20 (6), 872–884. https://doi.org/10.1631/FITEE.1800520.

Ren, P., Xiao, Y., Chang, Huang., P. Y., Li,, Z., Gupta, B. B., Chen, X., Wang, X., 2021. A Survey of Deep Active Learning. *ACM Computing Surveys* 54 (9). https://doi.org/10.1145/3472291.

Rožanec, J. M., Fortuna, B., Mladenić, D., 2022b. Knowledge Graph-Based Rich and Confidentiality Preserving Explainable Artificial Intelligence (XAI). *Information Fusion* 81 (December 2020), 91–102. https://doi.org/10.1016/j.inffus.2021.11.015.

Rožanec, J.M.; Fortuna, B.; Mladenić, D. 2022e. Reframing Demand Forecasting: A Two-Fold Approach for Lumpy and Intermittent Demand. *Sustainability* 14 (15):9295. (July 2022) https://doi.org/10.3390/su14159295

Rožanec, J. M., Novalija, I., Zajec, P., Kenda, K., Tavakoli, H., Suh, S., Veliou, E., Papamartzivanos, D., Giannetsos, T., Menesidou, S.A., 2022a. Human-Centric Artificial Intelligence Architecture for Industry 5.0 Applications. http://arxiv.org/abs/2203.10794.

Rožanec, J. M., Trajkova, E., Dam, P., Fortuna, B., Mladenić, D., 2022d. Streaming Machine Learning and Online Active Learning for Automated Visual Inspection. *IFAC-PapersOnLine* 55. Association for Computing Machinery. https://doi.org/10.1016/j.ifacol.2022.04.206.

Rožanec, J. M., Trajkova, E., Novalija, I., Zajec, P., Kenda, K., Fortuna, B., Mladenić, D., 2022c. Enriching Artificial Intelligence Explanations with Knowledge Fragments. *Future Internet* 14 (5), 1–11. https://doi.org/10.3390/fi14050134.

Settles, B., 2010. Active Learning Literature Survey. *Computer Sciences Technical Report 1648*. https://doi.org/10.1016/j.matlet.2010.11.072.

Seung, H. S., Opper, M., Sompolinsky, H., 1992. *Query by Committee*, 287–294.

Shao, H., 2019. Query by Diverse Committee in Transfer Active Learning. *Frontiers of Computer Science* 13 (2), 280–291. https://doi.org/10.1007/s11704-017-6117-6.

Shen, Y., Yun, H., Lipton, Z. C., Kronrod, Y., Anandkumar, A., 2017. Deep Active Learning for Named Entity Recognition. *Proceedings of the 2nd Workshop on Representation Learning for NLP, Rep4NLP 2017 at the 55th Annual Meeting of the Association for Computational Linguistics, ACL 2017*, 252–.

Shi, X., Dou, Q., Xue, C., Qin, J., Chen, H., Heng, P-A., 2019. An Active Learning Approach for Reducing Annotation Cost in Skin Lesion Analysis. *Lecture Notes in Computer Science (Including Subseries Lecture Notes in Artificial Intelligence and Lecture Notes in Bioinformatics)* 11861 LNCS 628–636. https://doi.org/10.1007/978-3-030-32692-0_72.

Shim, J., Kang, S., Cho, S., 2020. Active Learning of Convolutional Neural Network for Cost-Effective Wafer Map Pattern Classification. *IEEE Transactions on Semiconductor Manufacturing* 33 (2), 258–266. https://doi.org/10.1109/TSM.2020.2974867.

Sinha, S., Ebrahimi, S., Darrell, T., 2019. Variational Adversarial Active Learning' *Proceedings of the IEEE International Conference on Computer Vision* 2019-October: 5971–5980. https://doi.org/10.1109/ICCV.2019.00607.

Sugiyama, M., Kawanabe, M., 2013. *Machine Learning in Non-Stationary Environments*. https://doi.org/10.7551/mitpress/ 9780262017091.001.0001.

Taylor, A. T., Berrueta, T. A., Murphey, T. D., 2021. Active Learning in Robotics: A Review of Control Principles. *Mechatronics* 77. https://doi.org/10.1016/j.mechatronics.2021.102576.

Tong, S., Chang, E., 2001. Support Vector Machine Active Learning for Image Retrieval. *Proceedings of the Ninth ACM International Conference on Multimedia - MULTIMEDIA '01* 54 (C), 1–12.

Trajkova, E., Rožanec, J. M., Dam, P., Fortuna, B., Mladenić, D., 2021. Active Learning for Automated Visual Inspection of Manufactured Products. *Ljubljana '21: Slovenian KDD Conference on Data Mining and Data Warehouses, October, 2021, Ljubljana, Slovenia*. Association for Computing Machinery. http://arxiv.org/abs/2109.02469.

Wang, Z., Ye, J., 2015. Querying Discriminative and Representative Samples for Batch Mode Active Learning. *ACM Transactions on Knowledge Discovery from Data* 9 (3), 17. https://doi.org/10.1145/2700408.

Weigl, E., Wolfgang, H., Lughofer, E., Radauer, T., Eitzinger, C., 2016. On Improving Performance of Surface Inspection Systems by Online Active Learning and Flexible Classifier Updates. *Machine Vision and Applications* 27 (1), 103–27. https://doi.org/10.1007/s00138-015-0731-9.

Wu, D., 2019. Pool-Based Sequential Active Learning for Regression. *IEEE Transactions on Neural Networks and Learning Systems* 30 (5), 1348–1359. https://doi.org/10.1109/TNNLS.2018.2868649.

Wu, D., Lawhern, V. J., Gordon, S., Lance, B. J., Lin, C. T., 2016. Offline EEG-Based Driver Drowsiness Estimation Using Enhanced Batch-Mode Active Learning (EBMAL) for Regression. *2016 IEEE International Conference on Systems, Man, and Cybernetics, SMC 2016 - Conference Proceedings*, 730–736. https://doi.org/10.1109/SMC.2016.7844328.

Wu, X., Chen, C., Zhong, M., Wang, J., Shi, J., 2021. COVID-AL: The Diagnosis of COVID-19 with Deep Active Learning. *Medical Image Analysis* 68, 101913. https://doi.org/10.1016/j.media.2020.101913.

Xie, B., Shen, G., Guo, C., Cui, Y., 2021. The Named Entity Recognition of Chinese Cybersecurity Using an Active Learning Strategy. *Wireless Communications and Mobile Computing* 2021. https://doi.org/10.1155/2021/6629591.

Xu, Z., Yu, K., Trespo, V., Xu, X., Wang, J., 2003. Representative Sampling for Text Classification. *Advances in Information Retrieval. ECIR 2003. Lecture Notes in Computer Science* 2633, 1–15.

Yang, L., Hanneke, S., Carbonell, J., 2013. A Theory of Transfer Learning with Applications to Active Learning. *Machine Learning* 90 (2), 161–189. https://doi.org/10.1007/s10994-012-5310-y.

Yu, H., Kim, S., 2010. Passive Sampling for Regression. *Proceedings - IEEE International Conference on Data Mining, ICDM*, 1151–1156. https://doi.org/10.1109/ICDM.2010.9.

Zajec, P., Rožanec, J.M., Trajkova, E., Novalija, I., Kenda, K., Fortuna, B., Mladenić, D., 2021. Help Me Learn! Architecture and Strategies to Combine Recommendations and Active Learning in Manufacturing. *Information (Switzerland)* 12 (11), 1–27. https://doi.org/10.3390/info12110473.

Zhang, T., Oles, F., 2000. The Value of Unlabeled Data for Classification Problems. *Proceedings of the Seventeenth International Conference on Machine Learning* (ICML'00), 1191-1198.

Zhao, Y., Chen, D., Xie, H., Zhang, S., Gu, L., 2019. Mammographic Image Classification System via Active Learning. *Journal of Medical and Biological Engineering* 39 (4), 569–82. https://doi.org/10.1007/s40846-018-0437-3.

Zhu, D., Li, Z., Wang, X., Gong, B., Yang, T., 2019. A Robust Zero-Sum Game Framework for Pool-Based Active Learning. *AISTATS 2019 - 22nd International Conference on Artificial Intelligence and Statistics* 89.

Zhu, J. J., Bento, j., 2017. *Generative Adversarial Active Learning*, 1–11. http://arxiv.org/abs/1702.07956.

Zhu, X., Ghahramani, Z., Lafferty, J., 2003. Semi-Supervised Learning Using Gaussian Fields and Harmonic Functions. *Proceedings, Twentieth International Conference on Machine Learning* 2 (2001), 912–919.

Chapter 7

Prediction of General Anxiety Disorder Using Machine Learning Techniques

Kevser Şahinbaş[*]

Management Information Systems, Istanbul Medipol University,
Istanbul, Turkey

Abstract

Today, the increase in mental health problems, the variable nature of mental health and the lack of sufficient number of mental health professionals have led to the search for machine learning that applied to mental health problems extensively, and its use in the field of health is considered as a new hope. Mental disorders are a health illness that affects a person's emotions, reasoning, and social interaction. Early diagnosis and the application of the right treatment after the correct diagnosis have always been the expectation of all humanity. As technologies develop, machine learning has started to attract attention in the field of medicine with the development of diagnostic methods. The aim of this study is to conduct classification studies by using machine learning methods in the diagnosis process of anxiety disorder diseases. A publicly available dataset of 672 people's Generalized Anxiety Disorder 7-item (GAD-7) responses during the COVID-19 period is used. This study demonstrates that it is possible to classify mental health status with 0.97 accuracy rates with the Support Vector Machine algorithm, which has a higher performance than other algorithms.

Keywords: general anxiety disorder, machine learning, data management, classification

---

[*] Corresponding Author's Email: ksahinbas@medipol.edu.tr.

In: The Future of Data Mining
Editor: Cem Ufuk Baytar
ISBN: 979-8-88697-250-4
© 2022 Nova Science Publishers, Inc.

Introduction

Machine learning is increasingly becoming a part of digital medicine and contributing to mental health research and practice. Machine learning can improve diagnosis, monitoring, treatment, disease outcomes and rebalance clinician workload. Anxiety disorders are one of the mental health problems. In this respect, this study focuses on the prediction of anxiety disorders. The aim of this study is to present a model that predicts anxiety disorder status in the population of Bangladesh during the COVID-19 pandemic in terms of GAD-7 score (Spitzer et al., 2006). This score is a symptom severity evaluation and screening tool for the four most common anxiety disorders: panic disorder, generalized anxiety disorder, social phobia, and post-traumatic stress disorder, in primary care and mental health settings. On criteria like work productivity and healthcare utilization, higher GAD-7 scores are linked to disability and functional impairment. The severity of initial symptoms is determined objectively and can be used to track symptom changes or the effects of treatment over time.

COVID-19 has become a worry in developing nations like Bangladesh, where the population is dense, and the health-care infrastructure is failing. People were afraid due to a lack of protective and control capabilities. Furthermore, they were losing money as a result of the emergency lockdown (Bodrud-Doza, Shammi, Bahlman, Islam, & Rahman, 2020). Data suggests that those confined in isolation or quarantine endure significant distress, including anxiety, rage, bewilderment, and posttraumatic stress symptoms (Brooks et al., 2020).

Early detection of mental health is a vital strategy for preventing and responding to serious s problems and consequences caused by mental illness. In this respect, machine learning-based technologies are making important contributions to medicine and care management in various aspects. According to many evidences, machine learning frameworks have the ability to speed up the workflow of clinicians and other care providers. During the COVID-19 pandemic period, a research of the Bangladeshi population's overall mental health was conducted. The major goal of this study was to use survey questions to predict anxiety disorder in people.

This chapter has following sections. The literature review follows the introduction section and summarizes studies on mental health issues. The background section provides information on the problem of mental health prediction. The Materials and Methods section contains detailed analyses of various ML algorithms such as Support Vector Machine (SVM), Decision

Tree (DT), Artificial Neural Network (ANN), K-Nearest Neighbor (KNN), and Random Forest (RF). All algorithms' analytical results are compared, and the algorithm that obtains the best result is selected as the model. Finally, the Results and Discussion section will go over the ML algorithms that have been utilized to predict mental health concerns.

Literature Review

Xiong et al. (Xiong et al. 2021) proposed a model that apply Ensemble based Bayesian Neural Network to predict three disorder by YODA dataset that achieved 0.90 accuracy performance for Social Anxiety Disorder. In the (Chekroud et al., 2016), the clinical remission from a 12-week regimen of citalopram was predicted using a ML algorithm. The data was gathered from 1949 patients that suffer from level 1 depression with 25 variables to achieve good performance. Their model achieved 64.6% accuracy rate by applying the gradient boosting approach.

Ahmed et al. (Ahmed et al., 2020) presented a model for distinguishing intensity level of the anxiety and depression at an early age by psychological testing and some commonly used ML algorithms, namely CNN, KNearest Neighbour, SVM and linear discriminant analysis. CNN obtained the best classification performance with 96.8% for depression and 95% for anxiety. Hilbert et al. (Hilbert et al., 2017) detected difficult cases from healthy cased and GAD disorders from major depression by applying ML algorithms. They used Binary SVM algorithm and achieved 90.10% accuracy.

Sau and Bhakta (Sau & Bhakta, 2017) proposed a model for detecting the anxiety and depression in elderly patient by using ML algorithms such as Naive Bayes, Random Forest, Bayesian network, Logistic regression and etc. They achieved 89% accuracy rate with Random Forest algorithm by using 510 geriatric patients. Tat et al. designed a framework to predict mental health problems in middle adolescence by using 474 predictors report and 7.638 twin's data from the Child and Adolescent Twin Study in Sweden. The authors applied ML algorithms, i.e., SVM, RF, XGBoost and Neural Network by SMOTEBoost that is one of the imbalanced learning approaches and obtained 0.754 accuracy rate with RF algorithm.

Ćosić et al. (2020) addressed the issue of mental health disorders prevention for healthcare professionals to predict a higher risk of chronic mental health disorders during the COVID-19 pandemic. An objective assessment of the intensity of exposure to stress and a self-report assessment of health care workers was requested by obtaining data from clinical records and hospital archives. The final stage included developing multimodal stimulation paradigms to provide neurophysiological responses. At this stage, the response to audio-visual stimuli was measured. Sensors such as fNIRS, EEG, EKG, EMG, EDA were used for reaction measurements. Built-in eye tracker, microphone and webcam were also available. It was emphasized that, unlike statistical methods, feature selection and ML classification discovered more complex nonlinear interactions. The study demonstrated formulability in terms of supervised learning, both regression and classification tasks. The neuro-physiological features retrieved at stage 4 can be found in a properly formulated supervised learning task such as RF, SVM, ANN etc. It presented a perspective with propositions such as its integrability with a model.

Background

Anxiety disorders are one of the most prevalent medical illnesses. Anxiety disorders are common at both the population level and hospital cohorts and are associated with a significant economic burden, poor quality of life, and a variety of adverse outcomes (Kanwar et al., 2013). Anxiety disorders are a common mental problem among teenagers (Rapee, Schniering, & Hudson, 2009). In addition to anxiety disorders due to general medical conditions, generalized anxiety disorder, panic disorder, particular phobia, social anxiety disorder and post-traumatic stress disorder are the five basic anxiety disorders, as well as their linked conditions (Karamustafalıoğlu & Yumrukçal, 2011). Anxiety is a type of affect with negative characteristics that distinguishes it from other types of affect. Difficulty breathing, palpitations, rapid breathing, trembling in the hands and feet, and excessive sweating are physiological symptoms that can be characterized as psychological characteristics including discomfort, excitement, emotion, and the fear of something bad happening unexpectedly. Some definitions separate anxiety from fear by limiting the source to the anticipation of an unknown danger.

Generalized anxiety disorder (GAD) is defined by the DSM-IV as a condition characterized by intense and pervasive anxiety accompanied by a variety of physical symptoms that causes significant impairment in social or occupational functions or significant stress in the patient (Karamustafalıoğlu & Yumrukçal, 2011).

Worry occurs almost every day for at least 6 months. It is about many events or activities and is extreme. The individual has difficulty controlling their anxiety. Accompanied by three or more of the following symptoms: restlessness, excessive excitement, or anxiety, tiring easily, difficulty concentrating or mind boggling, irritability, muscle tension, and sleep disturbance (difficulty falling or staying asleep, or restless and restless sleep) (Karamustafalıoğlu & Yumrukçal, 2011).

The high frequency of accompanying mental disorders makes it difficult to predict the clinical course and prognosis. Panic disorder is seen in approximately 25% of the patients, and major depressive disorder is also seen in 50-80% of the patients. Coexistence of depression increases the risk of suicide. It can continue throughout life (Sadock & Sadock, 2008).

It should be questioned whether the patient has been especially nervous and worried that something bad will happen in the last months, what his/her anxiety is about and whether he/she has been able to control his anxiety. Most patients' anxiety subsides when they have the opportunity to discuss their difficulties with an attending physician. The clinician can identify external situations that cause anxiety, change the environment with the help of the patient or their family, and help them function effectively in their daily work and relationships. Patients can thus reveal new rewards and pleasures that are therapeutic for them (Karamustafalıoğlu & Yumrukçal, 2011).

GAD-7 seven-item measure that evaluates symptoms of generalized anxiety disorder (GAD) showed reasonable specificity and sensitivity. This scale includes seven questions with responses ranging from 0 ("Not at all") to 3 ("Nearly every day"). The overall score was between 0 and 21. A total score of 0–4 shows minimal anxiety, 5–9 shows mild anxiety, 10–14 shows moderate anxiety, and 15–21 shows severe anxiety. Cronbach's alpha was 0.84 for this scale. Anxiety positive was assigned to those who scored 10 in this study score (Spitzer et al., 2006).

The diagnosis of generalized anxiety disorder should be investigated and confirmed by other methods for those who have a total score of 10.

Materials and Methods

The dataset used is described, the SVM, Decision Tree, ANN, RF and KNN algorithms are explained, and the experimental results are presented in detail in this section.

Table 1. Generalized Anxiety Disorder scale (GAD-7)

Questions	Score
1. In the last two weeks, I am feeling nervous, anxious, or on edge.	
Not at all	0
Several days	1
More than half of the days	2
Nearly every day	3
2. In the last two weeks, I am not being able to stop or control worrying.	
Not at all	0
Several days	1
More than half of the days	2
Nearly every day	3
3. In the last two weeks, I am worrying too much about different things.	
Not at all	0
Several days	1
More than half of the days	2
Nearly every day	3
4. In the last two weeks, I feel trouble in relaxing.	
Not at all	0
Several days	1
More than half of the days	2
Nearly every day	3
5. In the last two weeks, I am being so restless that it's hard to sit still.	
Not at all	0
Several days	1
More than half of the days	2
Nearly every day	3
6. In the last two weeks, I becoming easily annoyed or irritable.	
Not at all	0
Several days	1
More than half of the days	2
Nearly every day	3
7. In the last two weeks, I am feeling afraid as if something awful might happen.	
Not at all	0
Several days	1
More than half of the days	2
Nearly every day	3

SVM

SVM, developed by Vapnik, is a supervised learning method based on statistical learning theory, named as Vapnik-Chervonenkis (VC) theory and structural risk minimization, used for classification, regression, and pattern recognition problems in data sets where patterns between variables are unknown. SVM is distribution independent since it does not need any combined distribution function information about the data (Cortes and Vapnik, 1995). Here $K(x, x_i)$ denotes kernel functions, α Lagrange multipliers. The inner products of the inputs are calculated with the help of kernel functions. Lagrange multipliers represent the weights. In SVM, the output value for a sample is equal to the sum of the dot products of the inputs and the independent combinations of the Lagrange multipliers. The main purpose of SVM is to separate the vectors belonging to different classes from each other and to obtain the optimal separation hyperplane.

$$y = f(x) = \sum_{k=1}^{m} \bar{a}_k . K(x, x_k) + b \tag{1}$$

Decision Tree

In the algorithm created by Morgan and Songuist, sample data with known classes is divided into small groups with simple decision-making steps. With each division operation, similar data are grouped and classified by inductive method (Safavian and Landgrebe, 1991). The basic step in decision trees is to create decision nodes. While the decision nodes are being created, the best attribute should be chosen as the node for the tree to branch in a balanced way and for the classification process to be done correctly. For this, the expected value in the whole system is calculated with the "Information Gain Theory" revealed by Shannon and Weaver (Safavian and Landgrebe, 1991). The information gain is calculated as in Equation 2:

$$H = -\sum_{i=1}(p_i \log p_i)$$
$$Gain(S, A) = H(S) - \sum_{v \in Values(A)} \frac{|S_v|}{S} H(S_v) \tag{2}$$

pi: antecedent probability of class i
H: Entropy

Q: Sample space
Sv: Sample space subset

ANN

Artificial Neural Networks (ANNs), which were first developed by Warren McCulloch and W.A Pitts at the beginning of 1943 and inspired by the human brain, make generalizations based on the data at hand and can make decisions about the data they have never seen. Each nerve in ANNs has its own information processing structure and is interconnected with other nerves through weighted connections (Fyfe, 2000).

Inputs: $(x_1, x_2, ..., x_n)$ brings the information received from the environment to the nerve. Inputs can be added to the neural network from previous nerves or from the outside world.

Weights: $(w_1, w_2, ..., w_n)$ are suitable coefficients that decide the effect of the inputs received by the artificial nerve on the nerve. Each entry has its own weight.

Addition function: It adds the sums of the multiplication of each weight in the nerve with the inputs it belongs to, with a threshold value, and sends it to the activation function. In some cases, the aggregation function can be much more complex, such as minimum, maximum, majority or several normalization algorithms.

Activation function: The result of the addition is passed through the activity function and passed to the output. The output of the event function yi is defined as in Equation (3) when adapted by the input vectors x_i.

$$y_i = \begin{cases} \text{If } 1, w_1 x_1 + w_2 x_2 ... + w_n x_n \geq T \\ \text{If } 0 \; w_1 x_1 + w_2 x_2 ... + w_n x_n \leq \end{cases} \quad (3)$$

RF

Breiman introduces Random Forest (RF), a machine learning approach originally designed for nonparametric multivariate classification (Catani et al., 2013). Random Forest (RO) is a community classifier that collects the results of a huge number of decision trees by majority vote (Kulkarni et al., 2016).

Random Forest classification, which is a decision tree classification method, is an ensemble learning model in which more consistent results are obtained by using more than one decision tree. This method, which is used in both regression and classification problems, is a classifier that gives good results without hyper-parameter estimation (Breiman, 2001). This method, which creates more than one decision tree during the training, is input from the results of these trees at the estimation stage. It enables the data to be decided by majority vote (Breiman, 2001). This classifier gives successful results because it solves the overfitting problem. The Random Forest algorithm is created with 'n' decision trees. This algorithm performs operations in two stages. In the first stage, a random forest model is created. In the second stage, predictions are made from the created model with the help of a classifier.

KNN

The k-nearest neighbor method calculates the class label of the test sample with the labels of the test sample's nearest neighbours (Soucy & Mineau, 2001). While classifying, the distances of each data in the data set to other data are calculated. In order to determine this distance, k number of other records is taken into consideration for a record. k recording distances are the closest to the calculated point compared to other records. It is important to determine the k value because the k value is too small to affect the model very much. Although they are points of the same class, it causes some points to be placed in separate classes or to create a separate class for those points. Likewise, being too large causes it to be as if there is only one class, and dissimilar points are classified together. For these reasons, it is seen that the number of k influences the classification. 3, 5, 7, which refer to majority voting, are the most used k values.

K-nearest neighbor algorithm steps;

Step 1: The new incoming sample is added to the class.
Step 2: Look at k neighbours
Step 3: The distance is calculated using the distance functions.
Step 4: The closest instance is assigned to that class.

Performance Metrics

True Positive (TP) indicates that the actual class and the predicted class have the same value. TP value is found when we classify people without anxiety disorder as non-anxious disorder. True Negative (TN) are correctly predicted negative values. This indicates that the value of the actual class and the predicted class are the same. When we classify those with anxiety disorders as anxiety disorders, the TN value is found. The False Positive (FP) value appears when the actual class and the predicted class overlap. FP value is found when we classify a patient with anxiety disorder as non-anxious disorder. A False Negative (FN) value appears when the actual class conflicts with the predicted class. FN value is found when we classify a person who does not have an anxiety disorder as an anxiety disorder. While it is desired to increase the true positive and true negative areas, reducing the false positive and false negative areas shows that the classification performance is good. The following metrics can be calculated with the confusion matrix.

Table 2. Confusion Matrix

Confusion Matrix		Predicted Class	
		Non-Anxiety Disorder	Anxiety Disorder
Actual Class	Non-Anxiety Disorder	TN	TP
	Anxiety Disorder	FN	FP

The accuracy value, which is one of the performance measures of classification models, shows the ratio of correctly predicted data to all predicted values. It is obtained with the formula shown in 4 (Ögündür, 2019; Witten et al., 2016).

$$Accuracy = \frac{TP+TN}{TP+TN+FP+FN} \qquad (4)$$

Recall is the ratio of correctly classified positive data to total positive data. From the data of the model created using this metric, the rate of finding positive class labels is determined. Formula shown in 5 is calculated with (Larose, D.T., 2014):

$$Recall = \frac{TP}{DP+YN} \qquad (5)$$

Unlike sensitivity, the ratio of positive samples classified correctly with this criterion to the total positive predicted samples is measured by precision. It is given at Eq. 6 (Karaağaoğlu et al., 2003):

$$Precision = \frac{TP}{DP+YP} \qquad (6)$$

F1 value, which is a harmonic mean of sensitivity and precision performance measures, evaluates two different performance measures within itself thanks to this feature. This metric gives a single benchmark (Eq. 7). (Sokolova ve Japkowicz, 2006).

$$F1\ Score = 2\frac{Precision*Recall}{Precision+Recall} \qquad (7)$$

ROC is a measurement value that is frequently used in performance measurements of machine learning algorithms. It shows how successful the created model is in estimating. ROC is a probability curve and FPR on the x-axis, y. On the axis, there are TPR values. Each point on the ROC curve represents a sensitivity pair corresponding to a certain decision threshold (Karaağaoğlu et al., 2003).

Data Description

The dataset used in this study is is publicly available[1]. The dataset represents a one-of-a-kind look at mental health in Bangladesh's population during the early stages of the COVID-19 pandemic. The data were obtained from April 15 to May 10, 2020, when the Bangladeshi government implemented a curfew and quarantine. A total of 672 (381 men, 291 women) individuals from the

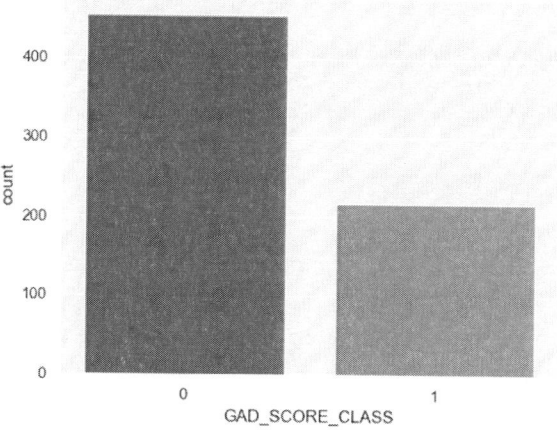

Figure 1. GAD score count.

---

[1] https://www.sciencedirect.com/science/article/pii/S2352340921006314?via%3Dihub.

Bangladeshi population aged 15-65 were included in the experiments and analysis. In this study, the sociodemographic profiles of the individuals were evaluated. The GAD-7 scale is used to assess anxiety. The questions in Table 1 were used to collect the dataset. Age, Gender, Marital Status, BMI, Occupation, Education Level, Residence area, Economical Status, living status, Smoking habits are features for sociodemographic profiles of the individuals. Questions are shown in Table 1.

In Figure 1, GAD score class is presented.

Normalization Filter

Large differences between the data affect the learning accuracy of some classification methods. The purpose of applying normalization is to facilitate the comparison of data by eliminating the differences between mathematical operations and data. In this study, the data were normalized using the Standard Scaler in the Python programming language scikit-learn preprocessing library in ANN, SVM, DT, KNN and RF algorithms.

Feature Importance

Figure 2 indicates the feature importance with RF algorithm. The results from Figure 3 show that the question "In the last two weeks, I am feeling nervous, anxious, or on edge" has the most impact on anxiety disorder prediction. Marital status provides the least contribution.

Experiments and Results

In this section, Random Forest, Support Vector Machine, Artificial Neural Networks, k-Nearest Neighbor algorithm, Random Forest classification algorithms that are frequently preferred in classification models, are applied to anxiety disorder data and the findings obtained as a result of the analysis are indicated in detail.

The classifier model techniques given were tested using Python software to determine the optimum model performance.

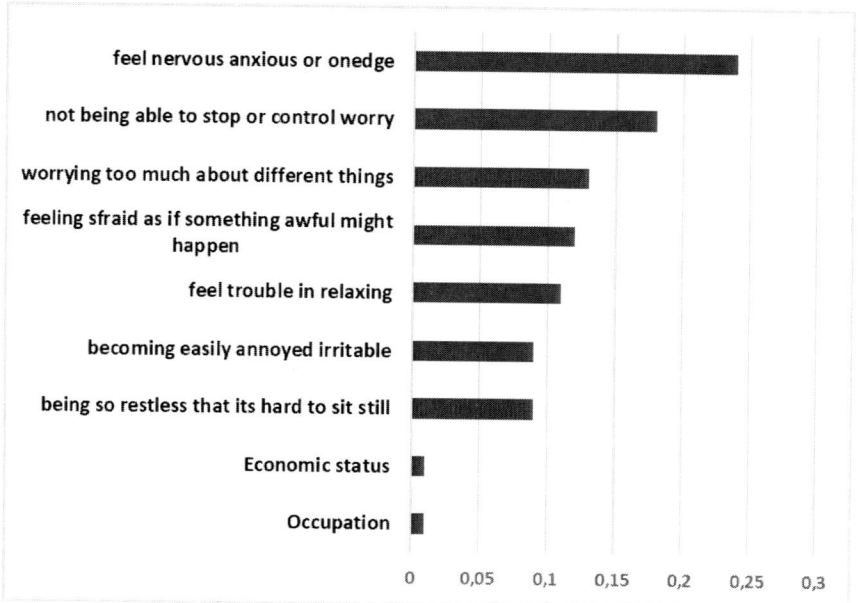

Figure 2. Feature importance.

ANN Results

In this study, multi-layer feedforward artificial neural network architecture and Backpropagation method, which is the most widely used in prediction problems, are used as the learning algorithm. The structure of the network is defined as a multilayer perceptron consisting of 17 inputs, 2 output data and hidden layers. 17 input sets are explained in the dataset section. The output set is to have anxiety disorder and not have anxiety disorder. The neurons in the hidden layer are between 50 and 100. Sigmoid for output layer and selu function for hidden layers are used as activation function. The epoch number is set at 5000. In ANN models, all other parameters are set as default values in Python software.

Table 3. Performance metrics of the ANN

Model	Accuracy	Precision	Recall	f1-score
ANN	0.95	0.89	0.95	0.92

Table 3 presents performance metrics for ANN algorithm. Accuracy is 0.95, precision is 0.99, recall is 0.95 and F1-socre is 0.92.

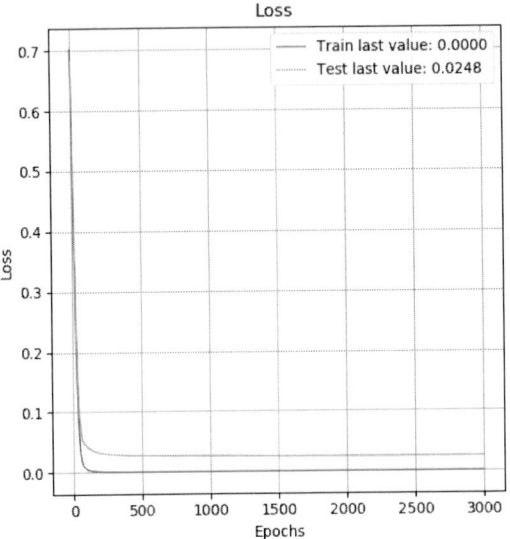

Figure 3. History of ANN.

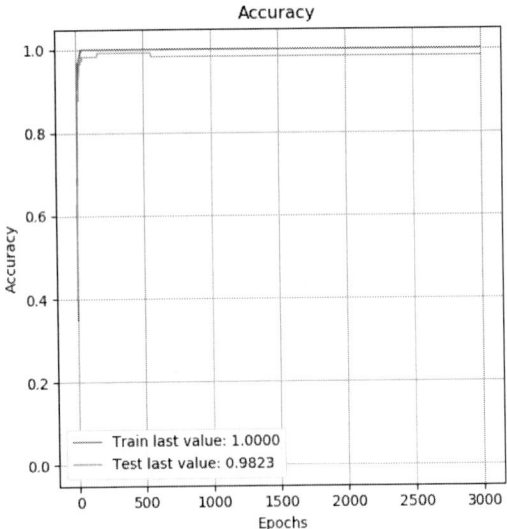

Figure 4. Accuracy history of ANN.

K-Nearest Neighbor Results

Table 4 provides KNN algorithm performance metrics. The accuracy, precision, recall and F1 score values are 0.88, 0.91, 0.68 and 0.78 for KNN, respectively. In figure 5, ROC Curve of KNN is presented.

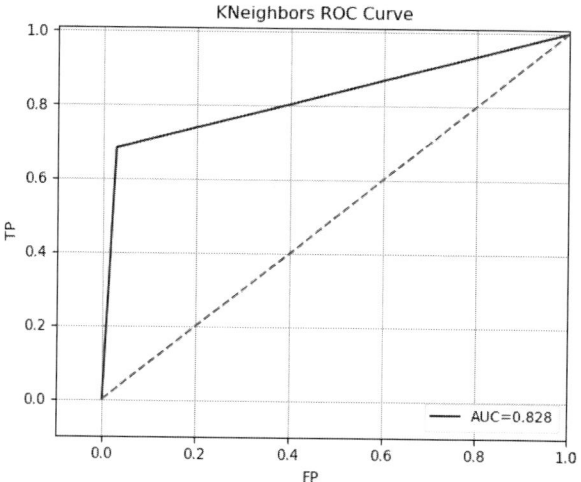

Figure 5. ROC Curve of KNN.

Table 4. Performance Metrics of KNN Algorithm

Model	Accuracy	Precision	Recall	f1-score
KNN	0.88	0.91	0.68	0.78

Decision Tree Results

Table 5 presents performance metrics for Decision Tree algorithm. Accuracy is 0.89, precision is 0.84, recall is 0.8 and F1-socre is 0.82.

Table 5. Performance Metrics of Decision Tree

Model	Accuracy	Precision	Recall	f1-score
Decision Tree	0.89	0.84	0.8	0.82

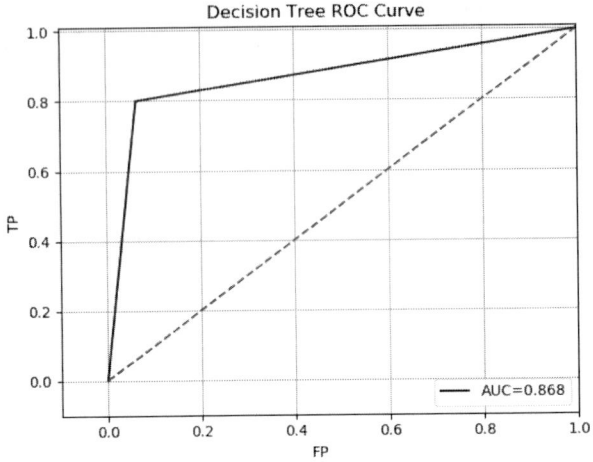

Figure 6. ROC Curve of Decision Tree.

Random Forest Results

The performance of the RF model is calculated, and the results are shown in Table 6. Accuracy (0.95), precision (0.93), recall (0.9) and f1-score (0.91) are obtained according to RF performance values.

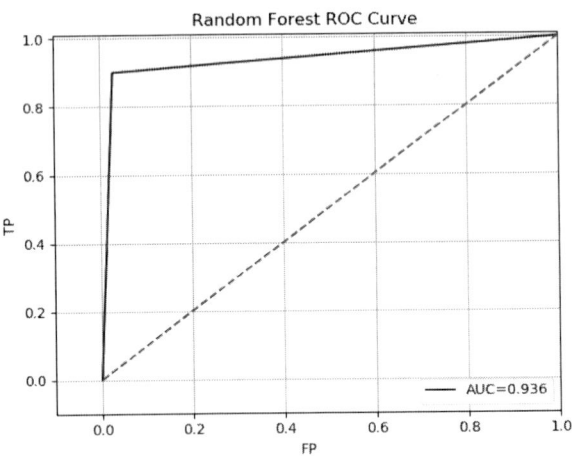

Figure 7. ROC Curve of Random Forest.

Table 6. Performance Metrics of Random Forest

Model	Accuracy	Precision	Recall	f1-score
Random Forest	0.95	0.93	0.9	0.91

Support Vector Machine Results

During the analysing of SVM algorithm, the feature values that give the best classification performance are adjusted (parameter tuning). The most ideal kernel and attribute adjustment are set by the grid method as a result of the findings. The Radial basis kernel is utilized as the kernel function in the SVM model, and the gamma value () is set to 1 and C (cost parameter) is set to 1.

Table 7. Performance Metrics of SVM

Model	Accuracy	Precision	Recall	f1-score
SVM	0.97	1.0	0.91	0.95

The results in Table 7 demonstrate that the SVM algorithm has an obvious advantage for anxiety disorder prediction. The accuracy, precision, recall and f1-score values of the data analysed with SVM are 0.97, 1.0, 0.91 and 0.95, respectively. The findings in Table 7 illustrate that the SVM algorithm achieves the best performance in predicting anxiety disorder. In Figure 8, ROC curve of SVM is illustrated.

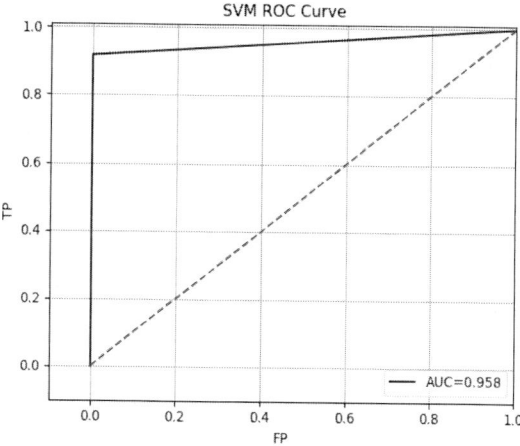

Figure 8. ROC Curve of SVM.

Comparison of Performance Metrics for ANN, KNN, DT, RF, SVM

The findings in Figure 9 and Table 8 show that SVM algorithm achieves the highest classification performance of predicting anxiety disorder with 0.97 accuracy performance.

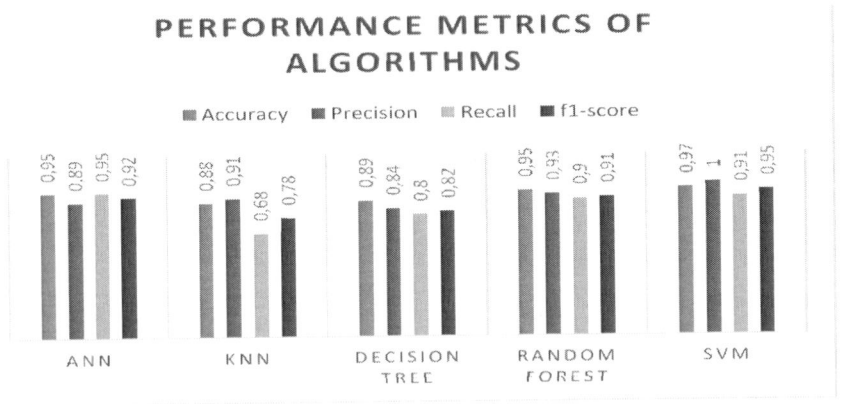

Figure 9. Comparison of Performance Metrics.

Table 8. Performance Metrics of Algorithms

Model	Accuracy	Precision	Recall	f1-score
SVM	0.97	1.0	0.91	0.95
ANN	0.95	0.89	0.95	0.92
Random Forest	0.95	0.93	0.9	0.91
KNN	0.88	0.91	0.68	0.78
Decision Tree	0.89	0.84	0.8	0.82

Conclusion

In this study, different ML algorithms are applied to predict anxiety. This research showed good screening properties for any anxiety disorder for the GAD-7 questionnaire.

To unlock the full potential of machine learning, mental health scientists, clinicians and patients must engage and take an active role in the clinical use, communication and collaboration of machine learning to help transform mental health practice and improve patient care.

The contribution of this study is to predict anxiety disorder by various Machine Learning classification algorithms. Besides, feature importance by RF is obtained. Among the algorithms which are ANN, KNN, DT, RF and SVM used in this study, SVM algorithm achieved the best performance with 97% accuracy ratio. The question "In the last two weeks, I am feeling nervous, anxious, or on edge" has the most influence on anxiety disorder prediction.

The fact that mental illnesses do not have a single cause, can be explained by many reasons, and the overlap of many symptoms makes the diagnosis process difficult for mental health professionals. However, with machine learning, it is expected that the automatic assessment of the diagnosis of thousands of people for psychiatric disease will be accessible by using artificial intelligence algorithms with a large number of data and digital health data records collected for years. Thus, a more accurate diagnosis process can be made possible in a short time. In addition, with the collected data, the prevalence of psychiatric illness in the population will be evaluated and appropriate preventive and preventive studies can be carried out. Besides, it is predicted that the collection of the mood follow-ups of the clients from data collection environments such as digital diaries will increase the effectiveness of the treatment process by providing continuous follow-up.

For the future work, it is planned to add additional mental health score and adapt the questionnaire to Turkey.

References

Ahmed, A., Sultana, R., Ullas, M., Begom, M., Rahi, M., & Alam, M. A. (2020). A machine learning approach to detect depression and anxiety using supervised learning. *In 2020 IEEE Asia-Pacific Conference on Computer Science and Data Engineering (CSDE)*, 1-6.

Bland, R. C., Orn, H., & Newman, S. C. (1988). Lifetime prevalence of psychiatric disorders in Edmonton. *Acta Psychiatrica Scandinavica*, 24-32.

Bodrud-Doza, M., Shammi, M., Bahlman, L., Islam, A. R., & Rahman, M. (2020). Psychosocial and socio-economic crisis in Bangladesh due to COVID-19 pandemic: a perception-based assessment. *Frontiers in public health*, 341.

Breiman, L., Random forests, 2001, *Machine Learning*, 45, 5–32.

Brooks, S. K., Webster, R. K., Smith, L. E., Woodland, L., Wessely, S., Greenberg, N., & Rubin, G. J. (2020). The psychological impact of quarantine and how to reduce it: rapid review of the evidenc. *The lancet*, 912-920.

Chekroud, A. M., Zotti, R. J., Shehzad, Z., Guerguieva, R., Johnson, M. K., & Corlett, P. R. (2016). Cross-trial prediction of treatment outcome in depression: a machine learning approach. *The Lancet Psychiatry*, 243-250.

Cortes, C. ve Vapnik, V., 1995, Support-vector networks, *Machine Learning*, 20, 273-97.

Fyfe, C., 2000, *Artificial neural networks and information theory*, http://index-of.co.uk/InformationTheory/Neural%20Networks%20And%20Information%20Theory%20-%20Colin%20Fyfe.pdf, [Access Date: 02 April 2022].

Hilbert, K., Lueken, U., Muehlhan, M., & Beesdo-Baum, K. (2017). Separating generalized anxiety disorder from major depression using clinical, hormonal, and structural MRI data: a multimodal machine learning study. *Brain and behavior*, e00633.

Kanwar, A., Malik, S., Prokop, L. J., Sim, L. A., & Murad, M. H. (2013). The association between anxiety disorders and suicidal behaviors: A systematic review and meta-analysis. *Depression and anxiety,*, 917-929.

Karamustafalıoğlu, O., & Yumrukçal, H. (2011). Depresyon ve anksiyete bozuklukları. *Şişli Etfal Hastanesi Tıp Bülteni*, 65-74.

Karaağaoğlu, E., Karakaya, J. ve Kılıçkap, M., 2016, Tanı Testlerinin Değerlendirilmesinde İstatistiksel Yöntemler/*Statistical Methods in Evaluation of Diagnostic Tests*, Detay Publishing, Ankara.

Larose, D. T., 2014, *Discovering knowledge in data: an introduction to data mining*, 2nd ed., John Wiley & Sons, Canada.

Rapee, R. M., Schniering, C. A., & Hudson, J. L. (2009). Anxiety disorders during childhood and adolescence: Origins and treatment. *Annual review of clinical psychology*, 311-341.

Sadock, B. J., & Sadock, V. A. (2008). *Kaplan & Sadock's concise textbook of clinical psychiatry*. Lippincott Williams & Wilkins.

Safavian, S. R. and D. Landgrebe, A survey of decision tree classifier methodology. *IEEE transactions on systems, man, and cybernetics*, 1991, p. 660-674.

Sau, A., & Bhakta, I. (2017). Predicting anxiety and depression in elderly patients using machine learning technology. *Healthcare Technology Letters*, 238-243.

Sokolova, M., Japkowicz, N. ve Szpakowicz, S., 2006, Beyond accuracy, f-score and roc: a family of discriminant measures for performance evaluation, *Australasian Joint Conference on Artificial Intelligence*, 1021.

Soucy, P., Mineau, G. W., 2001, A simple knn algorithm for text categorization, in: *Data Mining, ICDM*, 647-648.

Spitzer, R. L., Kroenke, K., Williams, J. B., & Löwe, B. (2006). A brief measure for assessing generalized anxiety disorder: the GAD-7. Archives of internal medicine,. *Archives of internal medicine*, 1092-1097.

Witten, I. H., Frank, E., Hall, M. A. ve Pal, C. J., 2016, *Data Mining: Practical machine learning tools and techniques*, 2nd ed., Morgan Kaufmann.

Xiong, H., Berkovsky, S., Romano, M., Sharan, R. V., Liu, S., Coiera, E., & McLellan, L. F. (2021). Prediction of anxiety disorders using a feature ensemble based bayesian neural network. *Journal of Biomedical Informatics*, 103921.

Editor's Contact Information

Dr. Cem Ufuk Baytar, PhD
University Lecturer
Management Information Systems
Istanbul Topkapı University
Istanbul, Turkey
Email: ufukbaytar@gmail.com

Index

A

active learning, v, viii, 95, 96, 97, 98, 100, 101, 102, 103, 104, 105, 106, 107, 108, 109, 110, 111, 112, 113, 114, 115, 116, 117
algorithm(s), v, vii, 4, 6, 10, 12, 17, 29, 30, 31, 32, 33, 34, 35, 36, 37, 39, 40, 41, 42, 43, 45, 46, 47, 48, 49, 51, 52, 54, 55, 56, 57, 58, 59, 67, 69, 70, 71, 72, 73, 74, 75, 84, 86, 88, 96, 97, 99, 101, 102, 103, 104, 107, 109, 110, 113, 119, 120, 121, 123, 125,126, 127, 129, 130, 131, 132, 133, 135, 136, 137, 138
analysis, v, vii, 2, 3, 4, 5, 6, 8, 9, 10, 11, 13, 15, 16, 17, 18, 19, 21, 22, 23, 24, 25, 26, 30, 33, 34, 41, 46, 48, 51, 52, 53, 54, 55, 56, 57, 58, 59, 66, 74, 75, 76, 82, 84, 85, 86, 89, 106, 112, 115, 116, 121, 130, 138
anxiety disorder, 119, 120, 121, 122, 123, 124, 127, 128, 130, 131, 135, 136, 137, 138
application(s), v, vii, 2, 9, 10, 11, 12, 14, 15, 16, 21, 24, 25, 27, 29, 30, 31, 33, 36, 41, 48, 49, 74, 75, 76, 85, 86, 95, 97, 109, 111, 112, 115, 116, 119
artificial neural network(s) (ANNs), 6, 52, 56, 58, 67, 71, 72, 73, 74, 75, 121, 126, 130, 131, 138

B

banking, v, vii, 51, 53, 57, 58, 74, 76
bioinformatics, 13, 14, 20, 24, 25, 26, 47, 112, 114, 115

C

churn customers, 51
classification(s), 6, 31, 32, 33, 34, 35, 36, 37, 40, 41, 42, 43, 47, 48, 52, 58, 67, 69, 76, 85, 97, 98, 100, 102, 104, 107, 108, 109, 112, 113, 114, 115, 116, 117, 119, 121, 122, 124, 125, 126, 127, 128, 130, 135, 136, 137
crowdsourcing, v, viii, 77, 78, 82, 83, 92, 93
customer loyalty, 4, 29, 51, 52, 53, 54, 55, 56, 57, 58, 76
customer relations, 30, 51, 54, 55, 56, 57, 58, 74, 75, 76
customer(s), v, vii, 4, 5, 10, 22, 29, 30, 31, 33, 34, 39, 46, 48, 51, 52, 53, 54, 55, 56, 57, 58, 59, 60, 61, 62, 63, 64, 65, 66, 69, 73, 74, 75, 76, 105
cybersecurity, 98, 109, 110, 116

D

data analysis, 3, 16, 49, 51, 52, 54, 55, 57, 58, 66, 75, 84
data analytics, v, 1, 2, 3, 4, 11, 12, 58, 92
data management, 2, 84, 119
data mining, v, vii, 2, 3, 5, 10, 11, 12, 13, 15, 17, 18, 19, 21, 22, 24, 25, 26, 29, 30, 31, 32, 33, 35, 37, 39, 47, 48, 49, 51, 52, 54, 56, 57, 58, 59, 67, 73, 75, 76, 77, 78, 82, 84, 85, 86, 92, 111, 116, 138
data preparation, 58, 66, 67
database, vii, 3, 5, 14, 15, 16, 18, 24, 25, 28, 57, 75, 84

Index

decision tree, vii, 6, 12, 30, 31, 32, 34, 35, 36, 39, 42, 43, 44, 45, 46, 47, 48, 52, 56, 58, 67, 68, 69, 70, 73, 74, 85, 107, 121, 123, 125, 126, 133, 134, 136, 138

G

general anxiety disorder, vi, viii, 119

H

healthcare, 10, 95, 106, 110, 120, 121, 138
human resources, vii, 1, 2, 7, 9, 11
human resources metrics, 2, 10

I

in silico, 14, 17, 18, 22, 23, 24, 25, 26, 27
industry, v, viii, 1, 31, 48, 51, 52, 54, 58, 75, 84, 93, 104, 105, 115

K

k-means, 6, 10, 30, 31, 36, 103, 106
k-nearest neighbor (KNN), 6, 121, 123, 127, 130, 133, 136, 137

L

learning from demonstration, 95

M

machine learning, vi, viii, 4, 10, 11, 34, 35, 47, 49, 67, 69, 76, 95, 96, 97, 99, 105, 109, 110, 111, 112, 114, 115, 116, 117, 119, 120, 126, 129, 136, 137, 138
manufacturing, 33, 95, 98, 104, 105, 110, 111, 112, 113, 114, 115, 116
microgrid(s), v, viii, 77, 78, 79, 80, 81, 82, 85, 86, 88, 89, 90, 91, 92, 93

P

prediction, vi, viii, 6, 20, 22, 26, 32, 48, 49, 56, 76, 99, 105, 112, 114, 119, 120, 130, 131, 135, 137, 138

prioritization, v, vii, 13, 14, 15, 16, 20, 21, 22, 24
promising, v, vii, 13, 14, 15, 21, 22
prosumer, v, viii, 77, 78, 79, 82, 84, 89, 93

R

random forest (RF), vii, 30, 32, 33, 35, 36, 42, 43, 44, 45, 46, 47, 48, 49, 52, 58, 67, 69, 70, 74, 75, 76, 121, 122, 123, 126, 130, 134, 135, 136, 137
robotic(s), 95, 104, 106, 110, 113, 116

S

software, vii, 3, 14, 15, 16, 17, 18, 19, 27, 32, 34, 35, 37, 39, 48, 52, 130, 131
strategy(ies), vii, 1, 8, 10, 19, 21, 29, 33, 34, 46, 54, 55, 56, 58, 75, 76, 79, 92, 97, 98, 99, 101, 103, 104, 105, 108, 109, 110, 111, 112, 113, 116, 120
support vector machine (SVM), 35, 100, 101, 108, 111, 114, 116, 119, 120, 121, 122, 123, 124, 130, 135, 136, 137

T

technique(s), vi, viii, 2, 3, 4, 5, 10, 11, 12, 13, 14, 20, 22, 30, 32, 41, 48, 49, 52, 76, 78, 84, 85, 86, 92, 95, 96, 99, 100, 103, 104, 119, 130, 138
tool(s), ii, v, vii, 4, 5, 7, 13, 14, 15, 16, 18, 21, 22, 24, 25, 29, 33, 35, 48, 57, 58, 69, 77, 78, 105, 120, 138
toxicogenomic(s), v, vii, 13, 14, 15, 18, 19, 20, 21, 22, 23, 24, 25, 26, 27, 28
true negative (TN), 38, 43, 68, 70, 73, 127
true positive (TP), 37, 42, 43, 68, 70, 73, 127, 128

X

x-means, 30, 31